THE MAGICAL GARDEN

Other Books by Sophia

The Little Book of Office Spells
The Little Book of Love Spells
The Little Book of Hexes for Women

Sophia's Web Site:
www.psychicsophia.com

THE MAGICAL GARDEN

SPELLS, CHARMS, AND LORE
FOR MAGICAL GARDENS
AND THE CURIOUS GARDENERS
WHO TEND THEM

SOPHIA
WITH DENNY SARGENT

**Andrews McMeel
Publishing**

Kansas City

00 01 02 03 04 RDC 10 9 8 7 6 5 4 3 2 1

Library of Congress Cataloging-in-Publication Data
Sophia, 1955-
    The magical garden : spells, charms, and lore for magical gardens and the curi-
ous gardeners who tend them / Sophia ; with Denny Sargent.
        p. cm.
    ISBN 0-7407-0500-8
    1. Magic. 2. Gardens—Miscellanea. 3. Gardening—Miscellanea. I. Sargent,
Denny, 1956- II. Title.
BF1623.G37 S66 2000
133.4'3'088635—dc21   99-055087

Book composition by Holly Camerlinck

ATTENTION: SCHOOLS AND BUSINESSES

This book is dedicated to my sister Richenda, who wisely says, "You can never have too many garden books."

and

To Elsa Sargent, a talented gardener and painter, who once said in a garden: "This is my church." These words have never been forgotten.

CONTENTS

Introduction

Why do people kiss under the mistletoe during the holiday season? Why are "forget-me-nots" called that? Why do some people burn sage to remove negative energy? What is "Deck the halls with boughs of holly" all about, anyway? In a word, magic!

If you have ever wondered what the hidden meaning of different plants might be, this book is for you. Plants have been used for thousands of years for magical purposes as well as for food and medicine. There are millions of stories and myths about magical plants, and they have been passed down for centuries within cultures and traditions and within families like mine. Here is a sampling.

Every plant has physical properties that we can discover by observation, but almost all cultures, especially ancient ones, believed that every plant had a spirit and a spiritual essence that could be used in rituals and spells to affect others and the world. Some plants are said to eliminate bad spirits; others, by their hidden natures, are said to bring love or prosperity. Some naturally curse people; others heal. Every culture has these plant stories and myths. Some are widely believed, even today; others have been relegated to "old wives' tales." Yet today, with the ever-growing popularity of natural medicine and herbal medications, people are once again remembering and seeking out the spiritual and magical nature of plants. This book is for those people.

In this tome you will discover curious legends, spells, little rituals, and bits of folklore surrounding hundreds of flowers, herbs, bushes, and trees, many of which are right outside your door in your (or your neighbor's!) garden. Although they are presented simply to entertain the curious, who can say if some of these magical items and attributes are true or not? Mint tea does calm one down and promote digestion, this we know, but does it also draw money to your home? Who can say? That is for you to discover, if you wish.

We do know that gardens heal; they cheer us up and make us feel good. This is the real magic of Mother Nature, the Earth Mother. She provides much of what we need in this life, and for that we should be grateful and honor her. Every time we lovingly tend our gardens and soak up all the wonderful living green energy surrounding us, we are doing so. Keeping this in mind is important.

This book is fun and maybe reveals a bit of the hidden magic lurking in your garden, yet you are the one responsible for all magic in your life—the power is within you! Plants may or may not help you in doing your will, but in the end, it all comes back to you. Remember the old law of magic, as real in the garden as anywhere else: Whatever you do returns to you three times over. Bring joy and healing to your garden and to your family and friends, and you will receive the same in kind!

Nothing is better than gardening and messing around with plants! Hopefully this book will let you look at your garden in a new light and maybe spread a little mystery and magic in the green shadows! Will garden magic work? Were the "old wives" and the ancients right? Find out for yourself!

Heal the Earth—rebirth!

—Sophia

CHAPTER 1

PREPARING AND PLANTING

To Get a Vision
of Your Future Garden

When you know that you want to put in a new garden or radically extend an old bed, but you're not exactly sure what it should look like, do this at night, and you will receive a garden vision. If done right, you will "see" what your garden will look like and what plants should be in it. This is best done at spring equinox, or on a full moon.

Go out to where the new garden bed will be and sit, facing north, with a cup at least half full of red wine. The moon must be overhead and visible.

Get comfortable and then move your chalice so the moon is reflected in the wine, then say:

DRAW DOWN, MOON!
DRAW DOWN, MOON!
GRANT ME A VISION,
GRANT ME A BOON.
DIANA THARNA,
BRING IT SOON!
DRAW DOWN, MOON!
DRAW DOWN, MOON!

Whisper your desire to see a garden vision. See the chalice filled with moon power, then drink most of the wine. Look deep, deep, deep within the chalice, and you will see your future garden—what you should plant and so on. When done, pour out the rest of the wine and thank the moon, then go to bed and dream of flowers.

SPELL TO GET A GREEN THUMB

Use this spell to acquire the ability to grow green things with innate talent and creative grace.

The Green Man is said to be the collective essence of Mother Nature expressed as active growing flora. His smiling leafy face can be seen in many gardens, in ancient church naves, and even in Roman and pre-Roman art. Some refer to the Green Man as the son, lover, and/or father of the Earth Mother. The spirit of greenery is a wise spirit to invoke into your life if you are to be a successful gardener, or so the old legends tell us. More and more gardeners are hanging representations of the Green Man in their gardens with great green results.

The Green Man was sometimes identified with Esus, the Celtic god of spring. Whatever his mischievous origins, the Green Man is the power lurking in every garden shadow. What every gardener wants lurks there as well, because everyone wants a green thumb, right? This is what one has when one "becomes" the Green Wo/man. To get his green-thumb blessing (a thinly veiled identification of one having the power of the Green Man), try this.

YOU WILL NEED
- a vine
- some grasses
- a tree leaf
- part of a vegetable or herb
- a flower
- a clay cup
- rainwater

THE SPELL
On one of the great feast days (the equinoxes or the solstices), go out into the greenery about your house and gather a vine, some grasses, a tree leaf, part of a vegetable or herb,

and a flower. Place them all in a clay cup, and put rainwater
in it. Let it stand outside one full day, from dawn to dawn,
open to the sun.

The next day, taste the water, then wash your hands
(especially your thumbs!) in this water and say:

> SUN AND WIND,
> EARTH AND RAIN,
> JOY AND GROWING,
> DEATH AND PAIN,
> AS THE GREEN GROWS,
> SO THE POWER GROWS.
> ESUS KNOWS
> MY BEING GLOWS
> WITH GREEN LIFE!

I am rooted in Earth,
My branches in sky.
I engender rebirth
As I live and I die.

Offer the rest of the water in a small hole in the middle of your garden—place the soaking plant matter there as well. Cover it with soil and plant some flowers or seeds over it.

Say:

I heal the Earth—rebirth!

And now, get to work gardening! You have the whole day ahead of you, O Green Wo/man.

Meeting the Garden Spirit

There are many spirits, it is said, that play in the garden, but one is most important. That is *the* garden spirit, the special spirit that expresses the soul of your particular piece of land, yard, or garden. It is traditional for the gardener to meet this spirit in trance or dream and receive marvelous knowledge about the garden. It is said the "Place Spirit" or "Genus Loci" can tell the gardener what things are needed, what pests are infesting, and other things about the garden. This spirit will also indicate what kinds of plants it likes and doesn't like, thus saving many expensive trips to the nursery to replace plants that "mysteriously" keep dying!

The way to meet the Place Spirit is to sleep in the garden or yard in question, especially at midsummer or near that time. If this is too much, then you can lie in the garden until almost asleep and then creep into bed with some grass or a leaf in your hand.

Before reclining in the garden, sip a cup of catnip tea or a small glass of liquor. Pour the last drops on the ground and call:

Genus Loci! Genus Loci! Genus Loci!
To me! To me! So may it be!

In the morning, write down your dreams quickly! Pay attention to them. You may always call upon the Genus Loci for advice and ideas after this.

BLESSING SEEDS

Seeds and bulbs have always been considered talismans or charms of life. They are the core of green growing things and as such are the very essence of magic. It is important to bond with your seeds and so prepare them for their roles in your garden with love. All things respond to love. To begin this relationship, it is traditional to keep the seeds in or under one's mattress or pillow for three days, and only love and peace can occur in that bed during that time!

In short, treat your seeds like your children!

It is said one should wrap them in white cotton cloth to bless them.

It is traditional to greet the seeds in the morning and tell them good night after your lights are turned off. During the three days they are with you, talk to the seeds and encourage them to grow and be happy and live up to their full potential.

Tell them how happy they make you and how you will bring them into your life. . . .

When you plant them, it is an old practice to shed a tear or two into the Earth where you plant. Just as children depart the home to grow and prosper, so should you see your seeds as your little green children.

Blessing a New Planting Bed

When a new garden bed has been created and is ready to be planted or an old bed comes into your hands to work in, this traditional little ceremony will ensure its fertility and health.

You Will Need
+ a feather
+ a piece of charcoal from a fire
+ a small shell
+ a smooth stone
+ a freshly picked flower

The Spell
Plant the feather in the east side of the garden and say:

GENTLE WINDS,
BLESS THIS EARTH.
FILL THIS BED
WITH JOY AND MIRTH.

Plant the charcoal in the south side of the garden and say:

GENTLE SUNLIGHT,
BLESS THIS EARTH.
FILL THIS BED
WITH JOY AND MIRTH.

Plant the shell in the west side of the garden and say:

GENTLE WATERS,
BLESS THIS EARTH.
FILL THIS BED
WITH JOY AND MIRTH.

Plant the stone in the north side of the garden and say:

> GENTLE STONE,
> BLESS THIS EARTH.
> FILL THIS BED
> WITH JOY AND MIRTH.

Drop the flower into the center of the garden and say:
> BY ALL THE ELEMENTS,
> MOON AND SUN,
> BLESS THIS GARDEN
> AND EVERYONE!

Leave it alone overnight and then begin planting the next day.

Asking for a New Garden

In many cultures, a garden is seen as a gift of the Earth Mother to the keepers of the home. It is something that you can't just make, but something that you have to ask for properly in order for it to prosper. Some areas are no good for some gardens; some are perfect. Here is traditionally how to find out if the Earth will work with you to create a vibrant garden in the spot you have chosen.

You Will Need
+ ten pennies

The Spell
Take the ten pennies and go out where the new garden will be. Go at midnight on a Sunday. Face east and visualize what sort of garden you wish to put in. Ask the Earth for a gift

of this garden. Promise to tend it well and not to ignore or abandon it. Offer the coins to the Earth by touching them to the ground as a symbol of your promise. Say the following and then toss them into the air above you:

In the air,
Over the sea,
Down to the land,
Erda, hear me!
I ask for a gift,
I ask for pardon.
Allow me to grow,
Grant me a garden!
If you so will
Give this to me,
Accept my gift
So may it be!

Then leave.

The next day, look for the pennies. If you find them all, then your offer has been rejected and the Earth will not give you a prosperous garden. But if some are missing, then the Earth has taken your gift and the garden is yours. The more coins missing, the better the blessing shall be!

PREPARING GARDEN TOOLS

My grandfather always insisted that tools had feelings and wills of their own. This meant that if you treated a tool well, it would make work easy and help you even when you weren't looking for help, but if you mistreated or neglected a tool, it might get angry and turn on you or get sullen and slow the work.

One should keep one's tools clean and orderly. Shovels, for example, don't really like rakes, and all the cutting tools should be apart from the watering cans and spades because they have different personalities. If a tool keeps falling over, it is a sign that the tool is not happy, and it should be moved or tended to better.

You must always sharpen one way, away from the handle, and always facing north. A little olive oil can be rubbed into the blades or points for good luck, then the tools should be left in the sun for a short time.

Once a year my grandfather would rub all the tools with a small magnet, facing north, of course. This is a good idea because it aligns the tools with the Earth and so the garden work flows easier.

The Moon and New Gardens

Keeping track of the phases of the moon is very important when beginning a new garden or redoing a bed.

Cutting sod for a new garden and removing it or pulling up plants that are not wanted should always be done during the last quarter of the waning moon.

Turning the soil and adding compost should always be done after the new moon, in the first quarter of the waxing moon.

Planting seeds should always be done in the last quarter of the waxing moon, and they should then be watered on the full moon at midnight with a prayer for bountiful growth.

For better germination, seeds should be soaked in water that has been out in the sun for three days. They should be soaked for a day, the best time being at the beginning of the waxing half-moon. Then you must plant them immediately.

Sorrow for Causing Harm

My grandparents always said that if you hurt a living thing, you should apologize and give energy to what you have harmed. So whenever they cut herbs, they would offer a little coffee or a pinch of dirt to the plants and apologize.

Before cutting up sod for a new garden, or pulling up plants to change an existing garden (weeds don't count, since you want them to go!), you should do something like I was taught.

You Will Need
+ a knife
+ a silver coin (or some other small object that you value)

Cut the sod or dig the earth with the knife and say:

FORGIVE THE HURT,
PLANT OF EARTH.
THOUGH THIS BRINGS DEATH,
THERE COMES NEW BIRTH!

Plant the silver coin or something small that you value at least a bit. Begin digging and pulling!

CHAPTER 2

SACRED
GARDEN
OBJECTS

SACRED STONES

According to the ancient Greeks, stones are the "bones" of the Earth Mother, Gaia. In every garden, stones are the key earthing points and elements. The art of stone "planting" is a complex and deep practice in Asia, where stones in a garden mark the flow of vital energies and the positioning of them creates special states of mind. Many such gardens have stones placed in the form of constellations, and this is said to bring the heavens down into the garden. Take out a star map and find your birth constellation or another favorite constellation. Gather the necessary number of stones, each representing a star, and lay out the constellation about your garden or in a special place to make this stellar garden glow.

If your garden is not as fruitful as you would like, place a tall phallic stone in the center on the first day of spring to bring more "yang" energy into the garden and so quicken the fertility.

Hindus, Buddhists, and Jews place stones while praying upon shrines, "prayer piles," and gravestones. Wishes can also be made in this way, and you may want to create such a prayer pile in a sacred corner of your garden. When you have a request of the divine or a wish to make, place a stone upon the pile and offer a small prayer. The power will grow in that pile!

Stones placed in a circle, spiral, or other primal pattern are said to concentrate the natural flow of Earth energy and so make a place numinous and apart from the mundane world. Surround special plants, small beds, or statues with a circle of stones to energize them.

Specially shaped stones express the powers of the Earth in special ways and should be treasured. Stones with natural holes in them grant wishes and should be hung up in a garden. Stones with faces are said to contain gnomes—powers of the Earth—and can be planted in the garden and asked for help. They are said to help heal ill plants.

Semiprecious stones can be added to your garden for wonderful magic as well! A hematite in the front yard protects from crime and any attacks, a carnelian buried under the entranceway prevents fire, a malachite brings money, an amethyst brings peace and spiritual powers, and a crystal brings healing and will become a positive focus for any energy, or so the legends tell us. Energize any stone by planting it at the base of a tree with a prayer for one lunar cycle.

Stones are the bones and the centering points of your garden; they are just as alive as the plants and flowers! Treat them as a valued part of your garden, and it will prosper!

STATUES AND IDOLS

Many gardens call for statues, ornaments, or little idols. Some are more propitious than others. Your religious beliefs may come into play here. Saint Francis is the patron of animals and gardens; the Virgin Mary, in all of her aspects, is a reflection of Mother Nature. Kwan Yin (the Buddhist goddess of mercy), Buddha, and satyrs are all traditional images that lurk in a garden and add that magical element.

A statue should not simply be dropped into the garden anywhere. Sit and ponder your garden. Close your eyes and open your mind. What beings want to live there? What images come to you? Ask your garden silently who should dwell in stone or clay within it? After this simple meditation, visit several outdoor statuary shops; more than likely, something will beg to come home with you.

Female or goddess statues should be placed in corners or grottoes or near water. Many flowers should be about them. Male images—satyrs, Green Man images, and so on—should be situated in woodsy areas, near trees, peering out of bushes, or amid vines.

If you want your statue to become a spiritual presence in your garden (a great idea!), then you need to bless and empower it.

First, wash it with a bit of salt and water to banish all other influences. Get a glass of special wine (or an appropriate tea) and bring it into the garden in a small cup. You should set up the statue where you want it and at dawn, midday, dusk, and midnight, on a special day, pour a bit of wine over the statue at each of these times. At each blessing, say an appropriate prayer or mantra. For a Buddha, you might say:

Om mani padme hum!
(Jewel in the center of the lotus!)

For a Kwan Yin, you might say:

Guan Shi Yin pu sa!
(Honor to Kwan Yin!)

For a satyr or a Pan, you might say:
Io Pan, io Evoee!
(Hail Pan, hail Great Mother!)

For a Madonna, you might say:
Ave Maria!

For other statues, do a bit of research; you'll find something appropriate to say.

When you are done at midnight, pray that this image blesses your garden and brings joy and peace to all who come into it. Burn a stick of appropriate incense and leave a flower on the head of the image. Close your eyes and place your hands on the statue. What do you see? Is the statue smiling? If so, your garden is now blessed with a new divine protector.

BELLS AND CHIMES

For thousands of years, gardeners have placed chimes, bells, and other wind-driven musical magical items in their gardens. Bells and chimes draw upon the kinetic energy of the very breath of Gaia, and this energy transforms into a new form of musical energy. Chimes and bells can warn, protect, soothe, relax, heal, or call the gods and spirits . . . so much depends on your intent and the kind of bell or charm you choose, as well as the material it is made of.

Steel or iron adds a martial, yang, or protective power to the garden. Bamboo chimes add a very soft yin or Earth Mother energy. Aluminum and glass chimes call the powers of the intellect, the winds and clouds. Copper bells or chimes evoke Venus and loving feelings. Bronze brings business, and silver calls money or psychic power. Maybe the purest spiritual sounds come from Tibetan "seven metal" bells, which are said to contain all the powers and influences of all the planets. Before you buy or make one, try it out. Close your eyes. What feelings come? What images?

What you add to the clapper is also very important. Many bells or charms come with paper flanges or wooden ones connected by strings to the clappers. To make your chimes call forth special magic with every breeze, draw, etch, or paint special symbols of protection, healing, or prosperity on these hanging flanges. A few possible runes might be:

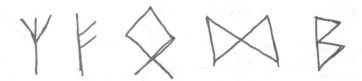

Possibly the most powerful thing to add to the flange of a bell is a feather. One special chant you can say when doing so is:

> WING TO ME, ECHOING SKY,
> POWERS OF HEAVEN TO ME FLY!

According to feng-shui, the Chinese Taoist system of energetic harmony, chimes and bells can completely change and improve the energy in your garden. Hang one over a "bad" spot and watch the vibes change completely.

To Bless a Birdhouse

You Will Need
 + a flower
 + some birdseed

After either creating or buying a suitable birdhouse, put it in the appropriate place and gather a flower and some birdseed. Sprinkle a pinch of seed about the birdhouse and say:

Here is now a house so fair,
Home to birds who are so near.
I bless you with the spirits green
To open up and now be seen.

Place the flower on top of the house, saying:

COME, O WINGED ONES, WE NOW INVITE YOU
INTO THIS HOME WITHIN YOUR SIGHT!
MAY YOU FIND IT NOW FULL OF DELIGHT!

Bow to the birdhouse and go. Soon it will be inhabited!

CHAPTER 3

THE
ELEMENTAL
GARDEN

Moon Plants

A garden is a very different place under the enchantment of a full moon. Just as the colors, warmth, and humid scents of a day garden give a wild boisterous joy, so do the pale, ethereal scents and sounds of a moon garden give a quiet meditative bliss.

The moon is the mistress of magic, and the ancient rules of gardening mostly fall under her divine sway. It is said that the Sun King rules the garden by day, but his divine consort, the Moon Maiden, rules by night. Certain plants and objects bring the lunar energy of Diana or Artemis into every garden. Some people even go to the trouble of planting "moon gardens" that flower and unveil their beauty only at night under the smiling moon. In such a mystical garden, anything is possible!

Some flowers—datura, nicotiana, jasmine, and gardenia, for example—bloom and spread their seductive perfumes at night. Others, like camellias, white lilies, and pale poppies, do not just open in the night, but can be planted to add pale lunar mystery throughout your garden. Any sacred corners or special spots that should resonate with the moon and her powers would benefit from such floral attention, especially watery spots.

Just as your garden has its favorite "day" spots where you play or meditate or rest, so it is important that you explore and enjoy your moon garden at night to discover the mysteries it reveals.

SPELL TO REVEAL THE
SPECIAL MOON WORLD

Here is a traditional spell to reveal the special moon
world of your garden to you.

YOU WILL NEED
+ a large silver or glass chalice
+ springwater

THE SPELL
On a full moon, fill the silver or glass chalice with springwater and stand before a moon plant that you have planted.
Raise the chalice up to the moon and "draw down" the moon
energy into the water with your gaze. When you feel her
power, lower the cup until you see the moon reflected in the
cup, and, from your heart, call the moon goddess into your

garden with whatever words you feel. . . . Then drink the water and feel the light fill you. Scatter the rest of the water as you spiral around your garden, offering the last drops to your moon plant. The moon magic will now always be revealed there for you.

Sun Plants

The sun is, of course, the source of all life, and certain plants especially embody essential solar power. They can bring luck, banish pests, and help bring the sun out from behind the clouds, as well as bring solar joy into our hearts and lives, banishing gloom.

Sunflowers have been sacred for thousands of years, and Inca priestesses of the sun goddess wore a gold image of a sunflower on their chests. Growing sunflowers in your garden, especially in the front of your home, is said to bring all sorts of good luck. They dispel pests and negative energies as well. Marigolds do much the same, but to a lesser degree. If you cut down a sunflower at sunset at the winter solstice, and then make a wish, it is supposed to come true before the next sunset!

Chrysanthemums are also royal sun symbols. Chrysanthemum tea brings solar power into your body even on the darkest winter day, and planted by your home, they confer royalty and confidence in the inhabitants. Give the flowering plants to people starting a new business to get it launched with royal success!

Heliotrope, though a dark plant, is said to contain the spirit of the sun because the plant originated when the gods transformed a nymph who was pining with love for an indifferent sun god, Apollo. Still the plant follows the sun across the sky. Heliotrope itself is poisonous and should not be ingested, but planted in the garden, it banishes all evil spirits and gloom. If you place some in a bag under your pillow, you will have prophetic dreams (Apollo was the god of prophecy!), especially if you want to know something special.

Spell to Make the Sun Come Out

You Will Need
+ a sun flower of your choice

The Spell
To make the sun come out after a long rainy time (this especially goes for fellow northwesterners!), do a small dance outside in the drizzle with the sun flower of your choice. Dance in a circle clockwise, saying:

Sun, sun, come and play!
Rain, rain, go away!
Kiss this flower with a ray,
Sun, sun, appear today!

Stand in the center of your circle. Hold the flower up and will the sun to come out! Bring the flower inside and put it in a vase on the table. Even if it doesn't work, the whole house will feel sunny!

Water in the Garden

Just as we are mostly water, so is the Earth. Water in a garden is the blood of life—without it, you have a desert. Water spirits love to play in a garden that welcomes them. They bring emotional release, relaxation, meditative joy, deep psychic power, and loving healing.

A spring or well is the most powerful water magic in a garden. Nymphs live in springs, and they have been venerated in every culture. Wells form special gateways into the other world, and ancient tales like "Snow White" hint at their magical power.

If a small creek runs through your garden or if you are living near a pond, the watery powers that gently sweep physically and energetically through your garden are gentle and revitalizing. They take ill or dark energies into their watery embrace and replace them with calm and ease.

If none of these watery energy sources are in your garden, then a small fountain, birdbath, or artificial fishpond is recommended. (Remember, certain fish, like koi (carp), are said to bring money!) This water source will be the "feeling heart" of your garden and should be kept up with clean vital water.

No matter what your water spot is, it should be blessed to maximize the power it can add to your garden. Special water-power herbs that are used in healing could be planted near your water spot. Some of these include lemon balm, burdock, Solomon's seal, and cress. All of these will conduct the healing power of water to soothe any angry or painful situation. A vase full of cuttings from these plants can do wonders in any harsh circumstance!

If trees are being selected for your sacred water spot, birch and willow are traditional. The best and most sacred flower is, of course, the lotus, but asters, water hyacinths, and irises are also wonderful water plants. Your water spot will be a great healing center for emotional and physical problems.

Blessing of a Sacred Garden
Water Spot

You Will Need
- some blue flowers (or a lotus)
- a stone from the ocean
- a stone from a spring or river
- a stone from a lakeshore
- a cup of springwater

On a full moon, bring the blue flowers (or a lotus), the three stones, and the cup of springwater to the garden.

Beginning at the western edge of your garden, slowly spiral into the garden clockwise, seeing the waters of the Earth flow with you. Stop at your water spot and drop the flowers in, saying:

FLOW IN, GROW IN, GLOW IN,
THIS LUNAR SPRING.

Drop in the stones, one by one, saying:

BY MAIDEN MOTHER CRONE
WITH EVERY BLESSING STONE.

Pour in the water from the cup after sipping it, saying:

LOVE AND HEALING BRING,
NYMPH OF WATER, SING!
IO EVOEE!

Silently commune with the water spirit. This is a good time to plant things at this spot as well. Then, spiral out of the garden counterclockwise, scattering the last drops of water in the cup. Leave by the eastern part of your garden.

FIRE IN THE GARDEN

Just as every garden has its sacred watery place, so too should fire be honored as the image of the spark of life from the fiery sun that is the basic energy of all living things. Many view fire as an enemy of the garden, but this is only uncontrolled or maliciously created fire. Fire, like water, balances the garden, but to protect oneself from unwanted fire energy, the garden can provide certain charms.

Two plants that are said to ward off fire are Saint-John's-wort and the larch tree. Snapdragons, especially if cut and placed before a mirror in the home, are said to keep fires away, and mistletoe hung by the fire in winter will keep the fire under control.

A place of sacred fire is recommended in a garden. Energy and power are needed for growth. It can be a fire pit, a lamp, or even just a simple outdoor candle lantern. One reason stone lanterns are placed in Asian gardens is to balance the elemental feng-shui—to provide a balance of fire energy with the graceful water.

Your fire spot should be in the sunniest, driest part of the garden if possible, with dry stones about the spot that have not been near a beach or river, if it is to be a fire pit. If not, one stone, as white as possible, should be set there. This shall be where your lantern is set. If the lantern itself is of stone, then this will do.

About this spot, fire plants expressing and manifesting bright solar fire energy should be planted. Some "fire trees" are alder, ash, rowan, pine, oak, and hawthorn. Some bright fiery flowers, which can be dried and displayed over the long, damp, cold winter to imbue your home with fire energy and warmth, are carnations, anemones, marigolds, yucca, Saint-John's-wort, fireweed, and sunflowers. Healing fire herbs that cast out melancholy and burn out disease that would be appropriate here include basil, bay, rosemary, peppermint, mullein, garlic, goldenseal, dill, and fennel.

BLESSING OF A SACRED GARDEN
FIRE SPOT

A fire spot is a place to get energized, to cast off the blues, and to fire your imagination!

YOU WILL NEED
+ twelve yellow flowers
+ a cigar (or a dried herb like sage)
+ a candle

To bless your sacred fire spot, and you certainly should, gather together at noon on a sunny day twelve yellow flowers, a cigar (or a dried herb like sage), and a candle. Light the cigar or herb. Circle the area six times, saying:

FIRELIGHT, FIRE MIGHT,
HEAT OF FIRE, JOY'S DESIRE!

Bring the burning offering to the center of your spot and then light the candle. Raise your arms and the fire to the blazing sun—see the light of the sun descend to empower your fire spot. Scatter the twelve flowers and say:

SUN FIRE, EARTH FIRE, NEED FIRE, BURN!
FILL US WITH LIFE AS TO YOU WE TURN—
SOL IGNIS INVINCUS!

Sit and be filled with the golden glow of warm life. Then put out the fire. Circle the sacred fire spot one time counterclockwise, seeing the fire energy sink into and enliven the garden. Return whenever you need a lift!

Living with Fairies

If you stand silently at midnight surrounded by ferns and you can hear no sound, then Puck, the most feral fairy, will appear to you and give you wealth—this is called "watching the fern" and is an ancient custom.

Fairies are said to live everywhere, just out of our sight, caressing the plants and helping them grow, quickening seeds and pushing roots. Where would we be without them? Why do some plants thrive in your garden, but others, against all reason, simply do not? It may be that the fairies for that plant are not present!

To make fairies feel at home (and so improve your garden!), plant foxglove, since the wee folk live in its blossoms. Also, plant hawthorn; not only do fairies love them, but they are also a very protective tree. A sprig should be placed over the entranceway of your home or garden.

If you want to see fairies, wear some thyme on you, chew a bit of it, and sit quietly in the garden on a full moon.

If you have an old tree in your garden with a knothole or hollow in it, you are very lucky! This is a fairy mailbox and, for hundreds of years, people have used these to communicate wishes to the fairies. On a new moon, write a short letter with your wish on a small piece of paper. Place a flower in it and put it in the hollow. By the full moon, they should give you an answer!

The Fairie Mound

Gnomes and fairies, sprites and brownies—whatever you wish to call the plant spirits—they will come and bring great prosperity to a garden with a fairie mound.

You Will Need
+ a fairly large (five to ten inches around) special stone that speaks to you of magic. Geodes are perfect.
+ some honey
+ a flower

When the crescent moon shows her face just after a new moon, plant the stone in the center or in the corner of the garden, be it a new or old garden. Place a bit of honey on it and the flower and sincerely invite the "wee folk" to come and love your garden. You might say:

FAIRIE FOLK, DANCE WITH ME!
I CALL THEE UP FROM BLOOM AND TREE—
BLESS THIS GARDEN AND RUN FREE.
COME, WEE FOLK—SO MOTE IT BE!

When you feel them near, dance about the stone three times clockwise, and they will follow you.

As long as the plant spirits or divas stay in your garden, it will explode with life! Leave them a flower or a drop of water or some crumbs about once a month.

At the full moon, spy on your garden, and if you are in luck, you may see them dancing about the stone, and you will know you are blessed!

Spell to Bring the Wild Folk into Your Garden

This spell is to attract wildlife into your garden, but only the wildlife that you wish to see!

You Will Need

+ a small rattle made with various seeds from your garden and whatever natural materials that take your fancy. Gords are great, but so are seedpods.

The Spell

When you have completed your rattle, hold it to the Earth and say:

GREEN MAN, GREEN WOMAN, GREEN CHILD, COME,
THEE THAT I CALL,
BY CRY AND BY HUM!

Then whistle three times to the sky, to the Earth, and around you.

When you are ready to use the rattle, be it at noon or at midnight, bring it out and hold it up, saying:

WILD ONES OF FOREST, OF EARTH, AND OF AIR,
COME FROM THY NEST, COME FROM THY LAIR!
I CALL YOU TO JOIN ME, IN JOY AND IN PLAY—
I PROMISE YOU SAFETY, BY NIGHT AND BY DAY!
I CALL AND INVITE _____ AND _____ AND _____.

(Here invoke only those critters you really want to share your garden with! Chipmunks, for example.)

> By day and by night!
> Bring to me joy
> In your delight!

Repeat this as a chant and, shaking your rattle, dance about the garden at least three times. When done, touch the Earth and see the wildlife coming. They will come, in the flesh or in dreams.

Set the rattle in a safe place or bury it in the garden at a special spot.

CHAPTER 4

THE PROSPEROUS GARDEN

Love Garden

Flowers are the most powerful love magic, as any courting beau or adored lady can tell you! There are so many flowers that are said to cast spells of love that it is impossible to note them all, but surely we know where to begin!

Roses, from the time of Shakespeare and before, have been said to cast spells of love on the giver and the beloved. It is important that the roses you use for such magic be free of chemicals and free of blemishes, a difficult combination! If you want to encourage a new love or the turning of a friendship into romance, use rosebuds. Use open roses for full erotic love. Growing roses by the front door or in pots on the front windowsill will bring love to you. Place them in the south part of the garden to bring passion, in the west part to bring emotional love, in the north part to bring forth loving commitment and fidelity, and in the east part to bring intelligent and thoughtful love. It is said:

ROSES PLANTED IN THE GARDEN SOUND,
SOON GREAT LOVE WILL COME AROUND.

Rose petals can be used for many love spells. Add them fresh or dried to teas, desserts, or dinners to cast love spells. Candy them with sugar and serve over vanilla ice cream to bring romantic love into the home.

Of course, there are many other love-inducing flowers in your garden! Periwinkle brings love and joy wherever it is planted; men should wear one as a boutonniere when courting! They will also attract the prosperity that wedded bliss brings. Honeysuckle about the posts of your home or garden brings commitment and devotion in love. Pansies are a token and charm of true first love, especially for same-sex couples, or so it is said. Columbine will turn a romance into true forever-love if it is planted in your beloved's garden on a Friday.

Daffodils are also powerful love charms. When a date comes over, have a big vase full of the cheery blooms right in the center of the house. When going out with someone you wish to love, pick a daffodil while saying his or her name three times, then place the blossom close to your chest.

To introduce romantic love to someone innocent of such things, bring violets, and press violets in letters or a book you give him or her. Candied violets or violet-flavored candies are also wonderful.

Lavender, when added to a bath with rose petals, will attract smart lovers to you. In all ways, lavender is powerful magic. It is said to inflame the heart, the head, and the loins as well! Lemon verbena, if drunk as a tea or added to a magical bath, will draw a sudden new love into your life—add some of the tea water to a new lover's bath or to a soup to hook him or her.

Other herbs that are said to attract love are bachelor's buttons (for men!), peppermint, marjoram, lovage, ginseng (for obvious reasons—it is famous for inciting amorous desires in both men and women!), yarrow, rosemary, and catnip.

Take the last three mentioned (plus any love flowers that you wish to add), dry them in the sun for one week (from Friday to Friday), and say over them each day:

I WILL TO LOVE,
I WILL TODAY,
SO LOVE MAY COME,
AND HERE IT STAY!

Then gather them and place them in a green cloth bag. Keep this under your pillow, and you will dream of your true love and bring him or her to you!

The strongest herb for love, legends tell us, is basil. To really seduce a potential lover, cook with fresh basil, or add it to some wine, or simply chew some before kissing! Scattering, burning, or eating basil is sure to lead to love! Scratch your lover's name on a basil leaf and carry it with you to entice him or her to you!

Some trees are also said to attract love. Almond trees, when planted by newlyweds, will grant a long and happy marriage. Birch trees are sacred to Thor and give strength to love as well as fertility, if it is desired! Hang beech boughs over the door or the bed if children are sought. Meet under a fir tree,

63

sacred to the feral god Pan, if you seek erotic excitement, but meet under a hawthorn if you desire marriage and faithful love! Another tree that guarantees conjugal happiness if planted is a linden tree, and maple leaves as well as the trees themselves are remarkable love charms. Stick seven maple leaves up on a wall to get love to enter a room. Myrtle planted about the border of your land will keep love in the home and concentrate it, while juniper, planted to the east, will attract love to your home.

But remember this, if you really want to have a wild love life, keep a new pinecone in your pocket; people will always be happy to see you!

Spell to Seek New Love

You Will Need
+ phlox flowers for planting

The Spell
If you are seeking a new lover, plant phlox flowers about your garden and keep six cut blossoms on your front windowsill. Replace them every three days, saying:

Over hill and over time,
True love, I call thee,
By phlox and rhyme,
Three times three—come to me!

SPELL FOR A SUPER LOVE PIE

Some fruits and vegetables are love foods as well, or so the ancients tell us. Oranges have long been seen as tokens of love; a gift of them means that a proposal will be coming soon. Plums and peaches are considered highly erotic fruit in the East and in the West, where they are said to energize the female libido and bring lust to an after-dinner dalliance. Beets are said to stir the animal passions and if eaten on a Thursday night, are said to attract the opposite sex the next day! But the most powerful aphrodisiacs and love charms in the garden, if the myths are to be believed, are apples and apple blossoms.

You Will Need
+ a double handful of apples, plucked by you on a full moon
+ a pinch of ground cinnamon
+ a pinch of ground cloves

- a pinch of ground cardamon
- a pinch of ground ginger
- a lemon verbena leaf
- a piecrust

THE SPELL

To create a super love pie, pluck the apples yourself on a full moon. When making the pie, add the cinnamon (air), cloves (Earth), cardamom (water), and ginger (fire), saying:

> AIR AND EARTH, WATER AND FIRE,
> ENFLAME WITH LOVE MY HEART'S DESIRE!

Add the lemon verbena leaf, mix the ingredients, and then top with the piecrust. On the crust, make the image of a heart with a fork, then bake the pie. When the pie is done, expose it to the full moon's light and repeat the spell. Then, when you are ready to serve it to your intended (or a friend as a "special" gift), mutter the spell one last time.

LUCKY GARDEN

We all have streaks of bad luck, and that is for sure. Who can say why bouts of bad or good luck sweep through our gardens like ill or balmy breezes? Many plants are said to be good luck, and your garden can certainly be both a source of good luck magic as well as a source of charms to turn your luck around!

If bad luck is haunting you, first you want to get rid of it. Burn a bit of sage, sweet grass, cedar bark, or oak leaves in the home and circle the garden as well with the burning herb. Place cut onions in your home to absorb bad energy, or scatter sea salt about and sweep your home well. Then you'll be ready to bring some luck in!

Place four vases with white lilies (or daffodils) in your house in different rooms or parts of the house, roughly to the north, south, east, and west. Alternately, you may plant lily or daffodil bulbs in the four corners of your garden. Do this on a

Friday when the moon is waxing. As you place a vase or plant
a bulb at each direction, say:

> LUCK, COME IN!
> ILL, GO OUT!
> LUCK, IN FLOW,
> TAKE ROOT AND GROW!
> BONA FORTUNA!

If you are looking for luck, let moss grow in your garden
and take a bit to keep in your pocket! The same goes for
clover, for it is said:

> WHERE CLOVER GROWS,
> GOOD LUCK GOES.
> WEAR IT IN A LOCKET,
> GOOD LUCK IN OUR POCKET!

Get rid of specific ills by placing one pin in a lemon for every problem, then burying the lemon at the foot of a pine tree at midnight.

Many a grandmother believes in the lucky power of a tomato placed on the mantel of the house. Pick it at sunrise, if you can, fresh from the garden. Keep it on the mantel for only three days. Change it for another one if you still need better luck! Don't forget to eat that nice ripe tomato, but be careful. Tomatoes eaten can bring passionate love as well!

Money Garden

Money, they say, is the root of all evil—but of what tree, everyone would like to know! Like all things in the garden, money comes from the fruit of the seed you plant: It can bring both good and ill to the one who calls it forth. If you have *real* need (not greed!) of money to make your dreams and your will come true, then you will see that money (magically speaking) can really grow on trees!

Just as they say it is better to give than to receive, so it is said that marjoram is an excellent herb to give those who are depressed and need money to come into their lives. Be careful, however, for it is said that to cook for a friend with fresh marjoram is to stoke the flames of love!

Many other herbs are said to bring wealth. Place four basil leaves in your cash register at your business and money will come rolling in. They can also be carried in your wallet or tacked up with a silver pin over your door.

Write your wish for specific money on a sage leaf on the full moon and keep it under your pillow. Success will follow soon.

Indians consider the root of the Oregon grape to be a great magnet for wealth if carried in the right pocket.

If sewn into a green sachet and carried over the heart, sweet woodruff should enrich you soon, and fresh mint can be used in all sorts of money magic. Rub some of the leaves on a ten-dollar bill and keep it with three fresh leaves in your wallet or safe to bring more cash. Scatter fresh mint leaves in your home and then open the door when you want more money to come. Wash the floor of any business that is losing money with tea made from twenty mint leaves boiled on a full moon, and all bad money luck will dissolve and customers will come.

There are many money trees that can enrich you. Oaks are said to give money, or at least acorns will. Find the largest, healthiest acorn on a living tree. Plant a penny at the base of the tree and take the acorn. Then, at the dark of the moon, plant the acorn at a crossroads, saying:

> Oaken seed of oaken old,
> Bring me silver, bring me gold!
> Llew of oak, here 'tis told!

Poplar trees have been associated with money for ages. Burn some of the dried buds or seeds and circle the house with the smoke. Soon money will rain upon you. A similar charm can be made with a piece of cedar or birch bark. On Friday at sunset, carve or draw the following rune on it:

Then keep it in a bowl or jar with silver coins covering it. You can burn it and make a new one every few months.

There are a number of special "money flowers," as one would expect. First, money plants should be planted near the front door, and arrangements of the dried "money" seeds should be placed on the mantel in the fall to attract cash.

Goldenrod flowers, the bane of hay fever sufferers, are said to bring quick wealth if planted in the garden or displayed in the living room. Where a small wreath of honeysuckle flowers is hung, money will soon come, or so it is said, and an onion flower, kept in the pocket, is supposed to bring quick gambling winnings—if you remember to quit while you are ahead.

Bananas and coconuts, sacred to the elephant-headed god of prosperity, Ganesh, bring wealth if kept on the windowsill with chants of "Gam Gam!" Pomegranates will bring treasure if hung in a house, but keep them out of the bedroom if you don't want children! Burn the dried peel and cense your wallet or purse to keep it full. Oranges are lucky fruit; giving them with a wish for wealth will bring good luck to a new business or family starting out. Keep six on the table in your kitchen and finances will stay positive. If you want a raise or to bring new money into your life, bathe in a hot bath with several pieces of pineapple peel and visualize gold falling on you as you do so. Do this on a Sunday in the morning and you will meet success.

SPELL TO BRING WEALTH

It is not surprising that many different food plants are said to bring money into the gardener's pocket. The surest way to wealth is to harvest the first sheath of wheat and braid it into a "dolly" and hang it on the door around the fall equinox. This can be done with corn husks from the first harvested ear as well. A simple braid is fine, with one end being the "head." As you weave, say:

> MOTHER HERTHA, WE THANK THEE.
> BRING GREEN WEALTH
> FOR THEE AND ME!

After you hang the "dolly" on the door, ask her for what you need as you open the door every morning. Burn the "dolly" when winter comes.

THE FRIENDLY GARDEN

My grandmother always told me that friendships were the most precious things you collect in life, and they are a lot like a garden. Some root and some simply wither away, no matter how much care you give them. And some just seem to come out of nowhere and flourish! Gardens are friendly places.

From the time of the ancient Hanging Gardens of Babylon, gardens have been places where friends gather and harmony and pleasure reign. Tang dynasty scholars and artists in China would gather in a garden and compose poetry or float small wine cups down a trained stream and discuss philosophy.

One of the most venerated plants in China, yarrow, is said to attract friendships and fraternal love. Yarrow stalks are used for throwing the *I Ching,* the most famous form of divination in ancient China, as well. Aside from planting yarrow in your garden to enhance friendships, you can also carry some on you to make new ones. Giving yarrow, either as dried flowers or as plants, will bind you to others and them to you in deep and faithful friendship.

Magnolia trees represent deep undying friendships. Wishes about friends or prayers for their health, it is said, are more effective under the magnolia's perfumed shade. Where a magnolia blooms, friendship always blooms as well.

To honor a friend and keep him or her happy, give daisies, cut or potted, for the garden or home. But if you want to find out if someone is a true friend, give bluebells; the truth will come out soon! If he or she is not a real pal, sweep him or her out of the house, plant some sweet peas, and get the pals you deserve!

The Sweet Pea Spell

Sweet peas, it is said, are guaranteed to make someone a friend or fill a garden with friendship. Plant them by your door to bring friends to your home! When planting sweet peas to attract friends, do so at sunset when there is a waxing crescent moon, and water them with a little lemon water, saying:

> From sour sweet,
> New friends I'll meet!
> To brighten my life,
> New joy I'll greet!

Spell to Ensure Remembrance

For centuries people have used plants and flowers to cast remember-me magic on others—to keep their image bright in the mind of a departing boyfriend or a waiting wife or an absent lover. Certain plants are said to plant that loving image deep in the mind, three of the most common being rosemary, forget-me-nots, and pansies. If you just want someone to think kindly of you or to remain loyal, give him or her daisies or orange or red lilies.

Forget-me-nots are called that for a reason: Give them to a pal or loved one who will be absent and he or she will always remember you. Plant them and whisper a deceased or absent friend's name and that person will be planted in your deep mind forever.

Here is a simple charm to ensure remembrance—and maybe faithfulness.

YOU WILL NEED
+ a long piece of grass
+ a piece of rosemary
+ a remembrance flower of choice

THE SPELL
Use the long piece of grass to bind the piece of rosemary with the remembrance flower of your choice, saying:

> ME YOU SHALL REMEMBER,
> ME YOU SHALL REMEMBER,
> FROM JANUARY TO DECEMBER,
> ALL THE YEAR THROUGH,
> AS I REMEMBER YOU!

Give the bouquet to your loved one before he or she departs. You will never be forgotten as long as you remember your beloved!

DREAMING IN THE GARDEN

Dreams can be merely entertaining or intense and prophetic. Many natural aids to dreaming can be found in the garden!

If you want peaceful dreams that are relaxing, place a vase of jasmine by your bed. If you are having nightmares and wish them stopped, place morning glories in the vase instead.

If you need to learn something in a dream, place a bay leaf under your pillow and ask for the knowledge. If you just want nice dreams, use a sachet of lavender. If you want to send a psychic dream to a loved one, blow the seeds off the top of a dandelion in his or her direction and project your wish, then go right to sleep.

If you want your dreams to come true, you can do one of two spells:

At midnight on a Friday, in silence, gather nine small non-spiny holly leaves and wrap them in a cloth. Place them under your pillow, make your wish, and go to sleep. Your dreams will come true.

Another ancient spell is to scatter marigold flowers under your bed, make your wish, and then say:

> WISH I WANT AND WISH I MAY,
> COME TO ME THROUGH DREAM SO FAIR!
> COME BY NIGHT AND COME BY DAY,
> COME, THOU WISH, AND BIDE THEE HERE!

CHAPTER 5

THE
SHADOW
GARDEN

GHOSTS AND THE GARDEN

Many plants have connections to the other side, so legends tell us. Gardens are favorite places for ghosts, and why not? Everyone likes gardens! Whether you want a ghost to leave or want to see a departed friend or loved one, plants from the garden can aid you.

A sprig of white heather placed in a special place of silence and meditation has the power to bring a ghost to you. After picking a piece of white heather at midnight, place it in a glass of river water in the darkest corner of your home. Sit and think of a departed loved one and it is said that the loved one's shadow will visit you.

Bamboo is a versatile plant of power, conferring longevity, quickness of mind, grace, and strength. In legends it is also connected with drawing the departed back to this world. Groves of bamboo in a graveyard can utter the whispers of the dead. In Asian countries, it is said that during the Festival of Honoring the Dead, ghosts can appear in mysterious moving groves of bamboo. Bamboo makes a powerful grave plant and ancestors can be honored through the plant.

Willows, especially near water, also attract wandering spirits of the deceased, and their long tendril-like branches sway to unseen winds late at night. Wreaths of willow are used to honor the departed.

If, however, you want to be rid of a ghost, then plant lilacs about your garden and bring vases full of the flowers into the haunted home! Scatter salt about the home, say a prayer of departing, and sweep the whole house. The ghost will move on. Garlic flowers and bulbs will do the same, it is said, as will fresh or dried sage, especially if some is burned.

Martial Plants

Sometimes in life, aggressiveness and intense action are
called for, no matter how distasteful it may be. Many plants
and items in the garden can channel intense feelings and
energies to help "fight the good fight." Other times, we just
want to unload our anger and frustrations, to let go of negative feelings, and the garden will be happy to help us with
this as well!

If you are involved with a real fight and you are clearly in
the right, and you need a dose of bravery, then wear a small
sachet of one or more of the following: yarrow, mullein,
borage, or thyme. Do so and visualize yourself as invincible
and brave!

When engaged in a dispute with a neighbor, plant juniper
bushes, pine trees, holly, ferns, or bamboo on that side of
your garden. Hang in the center of the bush or on the tree a

small mirror pointing at the offender and say: "Three times ill, back to you spill!" This can also be personalized by giving an offender a potted plant with a small mirror buried in its roots.

If you want someone to move who is of ill will, secretly plant garlic or rue in his or her yard—it is said that he or she will soon depart.

SPELL FOR INCREASED STRENGTH

When engaged in a real fight with someone, you should burn some dried nettle or thistle leaves as fighting incense. You can even give some to your opponent! Point a thistle head at your enemy and curse them; your opponent will feel your sting! Then burn the thistle. Write someone's name on a piece of paper in red and impale it on a thorn of a quince tree or blackberry bramble on a dark moon to curse him or her. Say:

> AS YOU HARM ME,
> BACK, BACK, TO THEE!
> YOU DO ME HARM,
> YOU'RE STUCK ON A THORN!
> LET ME BE,
> AND YOU'LL GO FREE!
> TYR!

Averting Evil

Your garden is your temple, your resting place, your party center, and, when trouble strikes, it can be your fortress and source of magical defense! Your garden is an extension of your life as part of Mother Nature. A real gardener is intimate with the Earth Mother, and a mother always protects her children!

When terrible things have happened or are threatening or when you or your family have been physically or mentally or emotionally attacked, the powers of the garden can help you to block the dark powers and so push away evil.

When under siege, place hydrangea flowers about the house and plant them in the garden. Hang wreaths or strings of red chili peppers by the door and about the home. Drink wintergreen tea and sprinkle it about the house. Place half-cut onions about the house and then after several hours bury them in the garden. Add as much garlic, freshly ground red

pepper, and cloves to your cooking as possible. If the trouble
is legal, keep a bay leaf in the right shoe at all times and burn
a bay leaf in the house.

SPELL TO AVERT EVIL

YOU WILL NEED
+ three small pine branches, a few feet in length
(or three fern fronds)

THE SPELL
   To banish evil that has come, go into your garden at night.
Cut three small pine branches, a few feet long, or three fern
fronds. Circle your garden with these slowly and call forth all
the powers and spirits of your garden in whatever words feel
good to you. Express your hurts and fears and ask for help
from the Earth Mother. Then "sweep" the house with these
branches or fronds, pushing all the dark energies out the front
door forcefully, saying:

Out! Out!
Avert! Avert!
Evil out is—
Alhiz! Alhiz!

Throw the branches away, off your property.

Dark Moon Magic

The dark of the moon is often said to be good for pruning, harvesting, weeding, cutting down, and performing other "destructive" acts in the garden that are necessary. This dark time is also a time of shadows and secrets in the garden. It is also a good time for storing bulbs! The best dark moon for this process is that which appears within the sign of Virgo, but any will do.

After the sun has set, at the dark of the moon, carefully gather your bulbs in silence and gently wipe them clean, then store them in a cool, dry place. Peat moss is an excellent storage medium. Say:

> Sleep now, children, keep thee well,
> By this simple dark moon spell!

They should be planted in the early spring; it is important that they be planted during the new moon. The new moon in Taurus is best, but any will do.

CHAPTER 6

THE
HEALING
GARDEN

HEALING GARDEN

Plants are, of course, the origin of almost all healing medicines. The garden in ancient times (and even today!) functioned as Mother Nature's pharmacy as well as her pantry. Millions of healing plants exist and even more are being found as I write this, and there are many wonderful herbals and natural medicine books available to provide you with remedies. Yet healing has always been an art that has focused on more than just the physical; the energies of the garden also promote healing of the spirit, the heart, and the mind as well as the body. Here are some of the magical plants, flowers, and trees in the garden that cast spells of well-being over the infirm, or so ancient wisdom tells us.

Herbs are the most common healing plants, and their fame is ever growing today. Saint-John's-wort, now a very popular antidepressant, was once also considered huge magic!

One should collect it on a Friday or, better yet, on a midsummer day when it is blooming, and place it in a jar with salt by the window. This will keep all disease "spirits" away. When with a fever, one should place some of this herb in one's pocket or under the pillow to break the fever.

Lemon balm is another venerated easy-to-grow healing herb used by the Romans and others. Bind it to a knife wound, and the wound will heal very quickly. Inhale the steam from this herb boiled in water, and all mental problems will fade away. It is also a love herb—soak a bit in white wine to get lucky in romance!

Burdock is a wonderful magical healing herb. Scatter the dried leaves on the floor to get rid of sickness or carry the root to keep plagues at bay! Fennel is another wonder; eat the seeds or drink the tea for any stomach problems. Wands made of the stalk were sacred to Dionysus and said to grant visions and be useful in healing rituals (they should be tipped with pinecones and wrapped in ivy). Plant fennel near you to protect from vicious insects or snakes!

If you know about vampires, then you know about the power of garlic. Today everyone loves this healing herb, and it still glows with some of its old magic power. From the Old English *gàrlèac*, meaning "spear" plus "leek," garlic was planted by Romans everywhere to protect and strengthen themselves and the land. Put it on the mantel or windowsills when illness comes and add it to bathwater when feeling unwell. It banishes all curses and demons, too! Plant it in the center of your garden to help all plants heal themselves as well.

Mullein leaves, if placed in a shoe, are said to prevent colds, and the herb is healing when soaked in a cloth and placed on the forehead. Plant it near the door to keep sickness away as well.

To make a magic brew with horehound, which is said to draw the illness out of a person, place five ash leaves and five horehound leaves in a white cup with boiled water. Place this under the bed of the sick person, and the illness will be pulled into it. The next day, carefully pour the brew out at the base of an ash tree and wash the cup!

Peppermint is a powerful charm to promote health. Rub a sprig on the forehead to banish all sadness.

There are many healing flowers that can work their magic as well. Make a simple knot in a piece of blooming honeysuckle vine and hang it up to cure a fever.

Red carnations are used in spells to give energy and strength to an ill person, but never to a person with a fever. For fevers, white carnations are suggested. Plant red geraniums in window boxes to promote healing; they are excellent gifts to recovering patients. Scatter them over the bed of someone who is recuperating and then toss the geraniums out the window before bedtime.

Gardenias are said to heal all nervous or mental ills. Dry the petals and scatter them about or place them in a sachet under the pillow to heal. A single bloom floating in a clear glass of water on a full moon will break any bout of depression or headaches, so it is said.

Of course, there are many healing trees as well. Rowan trees, ash trees, birch trees, oak trees—all of these and more are said to promote healing. To cast off illness, wash yourself and pour the water at the base of a tree—it will take your illness away.

Of course, simply sitting or lying in the garden will help heal you. Prepare a light herbal tea, inhale the perfume from a healing flower or herb, and let Mother Nature fill you with her healing touch.

Herb Healing Spell

Another great healing plant, around the world it seems, is sage. It is said:

> If you would live forever and a day,
> Eat fresh sage in the month of May.

From Indians who burn sage to exorcise negativity and illness to the ancients of Europe who swore that sage tea extended life, sage seems to be a fantastic power! Romans named it *salvus,* or "safe," because of its powers. To remove negative energies within a home where illness has been, make a pot of very strong sage tea with fresh leaves picked on the full moon. Set some of the dried leaves aside. When the tea cools, burn some of the reserved leaves and fill the home with the smoke after opening all the windows. Take the cooled tea outside. Hold it up to the sky and say:

Jupiter Pater, hear my plea,
Remove all illness now from me!
By the salvus sacred to thee,
Begone all evil, so mote it be!

Then sip some of the tea yourself and give some to the person who is ill, if it isn't you. When washing all the bedding and clothes of the ill person, add a half cup of the tea to each washing. Add to a bath to refresh and reinvigorate. Sprinkle the floors and other places with the tea until it is all gone. Bury the spent leaves at the base of a sage bush and thank the salvus spirit for the cleansing!

Granny Good Witch's Special Brew

My grandmother was fond of dried blackberry leaves as a cure. She said to use this for stomach cramps. We would make an infusion and say while drinking:

> Three ladies did come from the East,
> One with pain and two with relief.
> Out with fire and in with rain,
> Two ladies of relief will remain.
> Lady of pain will depart,
> Out with fire and in with rain.

This is a very old invocation to the ancient Celtic goddess Brigit.

Healing Garden Tree Spell

If you feel ill, fatigued, or simply overburdened, a friendly garden tree will always help you out, especially if you have a good relationship with it. Make sure it is well watered and so on, then, on a new moon night, approach your favorite tree and say:

> Old friend, wise one, tall one, tree,
> I who love you now need thee!
> From pain and sorrow,
> May I be free!

Take a leaf from the tree, thanking the tree, then rub the leaf all over your body, beginning at the head. See the leaf taking all the negative energy from your body. Say several times:

ALL THAT HINDERS, TO THE EARTH . . .

When done, bury the leaf at the foot of the tree, saying:

HERE I LAY ALL PAIN AND STRIFE—
TAKE MY WASTE AND CHANGE IT TO LIFE!
HEAL ME NOW AND I'LL HEAL THEE,
OLD FRIEND, WISE ONE, TALL ONE, TREE!

Water the tree. Then go back inside and go to bed.

Mind-Focusing Garden

Too often we let the frantic nonsensical world outside our gardens pull us this way and that—our concentration becomes as short and crazed as a TV commercial! The garden can offer green mental magic to focus the thinking and get one's brain straightened out and on track.

Near where you do the most sitting and thinking, or in a pot on your mental patio, plant periwinkle, otherwise known as blue buttons. These lovely flowers are very magical and are also said to attract wealth and protect you—but their main power is to clear and focus your poor harried gray matter! Another excellent plant that claifies and focuses the mind is lily of the valley. If you wish to plant an herb instead of or in addition to a mental-magic flower, try summer savory, rue, or rosemary. All are said to make one smarter and sharper.

Any of these herbs, especially summer savory, can also be put into a small sachet to be worn or carried when you need mental clarity away from your sane little garden. Cut the herb on a new moon and dry it in the midday sun on a Wednesday, then place it in a light blue cloth or sachet bag. Draw the symbol of Mercury on it for good measure. Take a deep sniff of it when you need a clear and focused head while visualizing clouds and a ray of sun piercing them.

Mental Clarity Spell

A great mental clarity salad can be prepared with ingredients that can be taken from your garden. Again, harvesting them on a Wednesday is best. Your mental-magic salad should include some of these: celery, grapes, caraway or caraway seeds, and fresh spearmint and/or walnuts. Bless the salad by holding it up to the sky and say:

Four winds, blow!
Cobwebs, go!
Clarity, grow!
One mind, glow!
Mercurius, fill me with perception
Four winds bring from each direction!

Green Meditation

Gardening can comfort and soothe the soul. The ability to just relax and enjoy the garden can be just about the best part of the gardening experience. Unfortunately, many of us just do not have time to center and focus in our silence and enjoy the garden and not to, dare I say it, actually do "gardening." We need more do-nothing meditation time in our gardens. Make a scared place or a quiet spot in your garden and practice this easy meditation.

Take your index and middle fingers and place them on the side of your right nostril, then close your nostril while breathing only through your left. Exhale, release your fingers from your nostril, and then place your fingers on your left nostril. Do the same on the other side. Practice this for five to ten minutes while focusing on your favorite spot in the garden. Feel the fresh air and garden as one essence flowing through you and your body, taking away all negative energy and leaving only the positive power deep in your soul. Chant this seed syllable to cleanse and relax your mind:

HRING. HRING, HRING. . . .

When focused and feeling steady, start to quiet your mind, relax and end the breathing exercise, and have a time of silence. The garden will talk to you: Listen.

THE GARDEN OF LONG LIFE

When a new baby enters your life, have it brought into your garden at midday and pass it three times through the boughs of a maple tree, saying:

> LONG LIFE PASS INTO THEE
> FROM THE BLESSED MAPLE TREE!

This, it is said, will assure long life for the child.

Ginseng, of course, is said to be a great all-healing tonic that will bring long life to all who take it. It is actually not too difficult to grow in a fairly temperate climate, and fresh ginseng is the best there is! Harvest at night at the full moon and cook with chicken to serve a meal that will add years to your life! If you carry the root, it is said to attract love, increase sexual potency, and bring beauty to you.

Sage is said to provide health and long life, as does the herb called life everlasting. Either of them can be made into a tea and should be drunk early in the morning before you eat. For a powerful tonic, hold a teacup full of any healing brew up to the rising sun and see it fill with solar life, then say:

> HELIOS BIOS,
> MASTER OF LIFE,
> REMOVE ALL SICKNESS,
> BANISH ALL STRIFE!

Drink this daily and live for many years!

Cacao Tree Protection Spell

Man's best friend may be a dog, but I believe a women's best friend is chocolate. The sad part is, we may be facing a major chocolate shortage or, even worse, the end of the cacao tree. Cacao trees are being threatened by a few very nasty diseases: Black pod, witches'-broom, and monilia are destroying our cacao-bearing trees. It makes us all live in fear of the seemingly impossible horror of a world without chocolate. What is a girl to do?! Sisters, we need to unite! Perhaps if we chant and visualize a cure, we can protect the cacao trees, and stop this from happening.

You Will Need
+ a chocolate cosmos flower (or a chocolate-scented geranium or your favorite chocolate candy)
+ a nice tray

The Spell

Choose one of the following to begin this spell: a chocolate cosmos flower, a chocolate-scented geranium, or your favorite chocolate candy. Place this on a nice tray, then lay it on the ground facing east and say:

> Cacao, mocha,
> Chocolate tree,
> May you be
> Healed and protected
> And disease free!
> Great Mother Earth,
> Let our chocolate be!

Now either smell the flower or leaf or eat the chocolate and visualize the cacao trees being healed from the roots up to the tops.

CHAPTER 7

GARDEN CELEBRATIONS

THE MARRIAGE GARDEN

If you want a wonderful and long-lasting marriage, then have your wedding in a magical garden and you will never be sorry! First of all, weather is important. If it sprinkles on you, this is great luck. If the sun shines on you, it is good luck as well. And if you see a rainbow, then your marriage will be truly blessed by the gods, or so it is said. Weddings are traditionally held in June because this is the month of roses, the most common flower charm for everlasting love. Always try to have some roses there. If it can be arranged that the bride and groom walk under a trellis or bough of blooming roses, their marriage will be blessed by Venus, the goddess of love.

Many other wedding flowers, of course, are wonderful! One flower charm that is often cited is a garland of violets woven by the girlfriends of the bride. If worn on the head, it will bring a joyous wedding and fertility as well.

Somewhere in the garden or the chapel, hang seven dried yarrow flowers (over the altar is best). This ensures that the marriage will last at least seven years, or so it is said.

If a wedding is to be held in the spring, a sprig of hawthorn should be placed over a doorway where the bride and groom are to walk. In fact, it is considered an excellent charm for a marriage to plant a love tree after the ceremony. A bit of the cake should be put in the hole first, with the bride and groom saying:

TREE OF LIFE,
MAN AND WIFE,
GONE ALL STRIFE,
UNITED FOR LIFE!

Almond trees, when planted by newlyweds, will grant a long and happy marriage. Oak grants stability, pine or fir incites passion, and hawthorn gives protection. Birch trees give strength to wedded love as well as fertility, if it is wanted! Another tree that guarantees conjugal happiness if planted is a linden tree, and a cherry tree grants joy and beauty to a union. Myrtle planted about the border of your land will keep love in the home and concentrate it, while juniper planted to the east will attract more love to your marriage as the years go on.

Blessing a Bridal Bouquet

One thing that should be added to the bride's bouquet, no matter what flowers are used, is a fresh-cut sprig of rosemary, the wedding herb. Cut it before by hand on a full moon, then place it in the center of the bouquet before the ceremony, saying:

To marry, to marry,
Hie thee, love, tarry,
With bloom and with bud
And rosemary for love,
Forever and a day,
So love will always stay!

Garden of Mourning

Every gardener knows that life comes from death, that the cycles of the year and the cycles of the garden are one, and that both include death as a natural part of life. Some plants have been magically associated with honoring the dead, and as such they symbolize the immortal, the cycle of life that is never broken, even by so-called death. In this way they represent transcendence and rebirth.

A hunter in ancient Greece who mistakenly slew the stag of Apollo was so remorseful that the gods granted his wish and turned him into a cypress. As such, this tree became a symbol of death and immortality, transformation from one life to another. In Greek myths, the gods of the underworld were always associated with the cypress. If you want to forever have contact with a loved one's departed spirit, plant a cypress tree near his or her grave. A cypress can also be planted in a garden or park as a remembering tree as well. The tree will become a gateway for communication with the departed. Wishes and requests can be tied with black thread to the tree, and offerings of wine or food can be left at its base. Sit near the tree and close your eyes. Call the departed's name eleven times while thinking of him or her. It is said that the ancestor or friend will be heard or seen.

Branches of cypress are carried at funerals as charms of both communion and protection. Cypress can be burned in a home where someone has passed on, and having cypress is said to help heal the mourning heart.

Yew is also a tree associated with the dead, and it is said that by placing a yew branch or wand on an altar or at a crossroads, one can summon the shade of a departed friend. If this is done, it must be burned afterward or the shade will follow you!

Beans have been associated with the dead and rebirth for thousands of years as well. In many cultures it was traditional to place beans in with the departed before burial; a handful is traditional. If you cannot go to a friend's or loved one's funeral,

it is proper to remember him or her by burying a handful of
beans in your garden. When you do so, burn a candle or lamp
and say:

> I salute _____ (name of deceased)!
> In the land of shade,
> Deep within the Earth!
> I send my love with this gift,
> That you find the light and rebirth—
> Fiat!

Garden Parties

Garden parties, in many ways, make the whole work of the garden come together. The garden comes alive with talking, joking, flirting, music, and a bit of chaos to spice things up! A garden party is always a magical mixing of the garden and the human. To make this alchemy successful, let the garden help you! Place little power plants from the garden into the thick of things by adding such power-party plants as peppermint, lemon, and nasturtium flowers to drinks, desserts, and salads. Always have a bowl of nuts in the center of the table, and offer one or two to the garden elves—it is said they will add humor and enchantment to the party.

Before the party begins, to make sure that the spirit will be festive, plant some sweet peas or sweet Williams about and/or have the flowers present in vases. Snapdragons will add pep and spunk, and lavender, dried or fresh, will add intelligence to the gathering.

Make sure all the statues have flowers decorating them, and, somewhere, hang a wreath of ivy, saying:

> IO EVOEE!
> IO EVOEE!
> COME, SATYRS AND NYMPHS,
> TO BLESS THIS PARTY!
> MAY WE LAUGH AND SING
> AND FIND JOY HOLY!
> IO EVOEE!
> IO EVOEE!

Alder trees and hazel trees are famous party plants, giving as they do inspiration and imagination. If you have them in your garden, make them a focus of attention for a successful party. Alder is the tree of artists, whereas hazel imparts the energy of youthful vigor and openness. Place branches of either of these trees about if you don't have them growing, or even burn some of the wood on a grill, if this is appropriate!

No matter what, have fun—play is the spirit of the garden—but watch those frisky guests when they're near the flower beds!

CHAPTER 8

THE MAGICAL ROUND OF THE GARDEN:

FLOWERS AND TREES OF THE TWELVE MONTHS

January

Crocus

The earliest flowers that come up in the new year represent hope, youthfulness, and new beginnings. The crocus, emerging as a quiet purple ghost, tells us to be careful, that life is fragile. Planting or giving these miraculous flowers (or bulbs) gives gladness and youthful happiness to others. The flower was named from antiquity after a shepherd, Crocus, who pined away with love for the lovely Smilax, and the gods changed him into this blossom. It is said that Zeus and Hera's wedding bed was made up of crocuses, and therefore it is a great blessing to toss a crocus upon a marriage or lovers' bed. The Romans believed its scent and power caused joy and strewed them about their parties. When you sprinkle them at a party or on a loving bed, say:

PHOS ES HEDONE!
ZEUS KAI HERA
HEIROS GAMOS!

Light of joy!
Zeus and Hera [king and queen of heaven], make it so
By thy sacred marriage!

If you wish to know hidden knowledge, burn some dried crocus flowers at midnight on a Saturday and watch the smoke carefully.

SNOWDROP

Snowdrops often emerge, like living snow, from the still-cold ground in January; thus they have been venerated as a symbol of new returning life for ages. They are said to magically give the psychic gift of recovering from sadness, and they bring new hope to the recipient, but never give just one or bring just one into the house—this is unlucky. If you want to cheer someone up (even yourself!) after a hard or depressing winter, place six snowdrop flowers in a small glass and say:

> TEAR OF ICE,
> TEAR OF SNOW,
> BRING SWEET JOY,
> BANISH SORROW!

Pine

Pine trees have been powerful symbols of life everlasting and hope through adversity for hundreds of years. Normally associated with Yule (Christmas), they have become associated with January because Yule once signaled the rebirth of the sun and thus the new year. The continuation of life as "Father Time" gives way to the "new son," or new year. In some countries, it is customary to place three pine boughs on your mantel and one on either side of your door on the new year to guarantee luck. When doing so, say:

Evergreen,
Ever living,
A joyous new year,
Full of giving!

Pine is a very magical plant with many uses. To keep evil away, use crosses made from pine needles bound together with red thread. Carry a pinecone for amorous adventures or place them in the bedroom to kindle flames of passion! Pine needles and boughs also get rid of all negative psychic energies. Burn a few and cense every room to banish winter doldrums and sadness, or place a small branch of fresh pine in a hot bath to cleanse and reenergize your aura, and to break any spells cast against you!

February

Primrose

The primrose is the first colorful flash of spring coming as winter fades away. Magically it has a mixed power, so the legends say, in that it represents inconsistency and fickleness. It especially imbues others with youthful folly, the ability to be a bit reckless and think short-term! This might be a great gift for the overly conservative or stick-in-the-mud friend who needs to be childish once in a while. Some old texts say that primroses cure madness, but they are also said to be associated with casual eroticism! If you are that sort of person, wear a red one on you and get ready for romance, but don't expect it to last! Several different-colored primroses can protect the garden from harm and invite good spirits as well. They are especially prized in small sachets as protectors of children. To create such a charm, take the blossoms of several primroses on Candlemas

(February 2) and dry them by the stove. Place them in a small piece of cloth worn by the child and tie it up with yellow thread, saying:

> PRIMROSE,
> HEDGE ROSE,
> PROTECT THIS CHILD
> WHEREVER HE GOES!

Keep the sachet in the child's pocket.

VIOLET

Many old tomes ascribe the month of February to violets, another sly but gentle harbinger of spring. Always symbolizing faithfulness, modesty, and loyalty, violets project a comforting and friendly magical power. Give violets, candied violets, or violet candy to someone you wish to be good friends with or to someone whose friendship you wish to preserve! They are traditional healing flowers, so give a potted plant to a healing friend or a bouquet of violets to someone recovering from a broken heart. Keep them in a living room or on a patio, wherever people hang out, and peace and tranquillity will prevail! Violets are also "luck turners" and when carried in a wallet, will change bad money luck to good, so give some to a gambler! They can also grant wishes, and it is said that if you pick the first violet you see blooming in February, your wish will come true, especially if you say:

> Luck to me, luck I see,
> Here is the wish I wish to be!
> (Your wish!)

Plum Tree

The plum tree, especially sacred in the East, is a powerful symbol of budding fertility as well as intellectual awakening and peace. Lessons learned under a blooming plum tree will never be forgotten, and poems or music composed or practiced under a plum will incite joy and wonder in the hearts of

listeners! For great luck, especially with romantic relation-
ships, bring a blooming or budding plum tree branch into your
home. As it blooms, so will love. Plum trees are said to magically symbolize longevity as well. Placing sprigs from a plum
tree over your windows will keep illness and old age at bay!
To gain patience and let go of irritation, sit or stand while
leaning against a plum tree, breathe in and out calmly while
seeing all stress dissolve, then say:

> SPIRIT OF TENJIN,
> HEED WHAT I SAY,
> LET ALL ANGER
> PASS AWAY!
> SPIRIT OF PLUM,
> TAKE IT TODAY!

March

Daffodils

Daffodils are really quite royal flowers as they lord over the spring garden with sunlike blooms and waving stalks! They represent the highest qualities of love, respect, and honor and are said to have been carried by knights and other gentlemen of valor, as well as royal ladies. In later times, they were symbols of the Annunciation, but they have symbolized the rebirth of the son or the sun for thousands of years. They are also symbols of reborn love, and they signal that courting season has begun. Give them to a potential lover to signal your affections and let the games of love begin! It is also said that gathering the first open daffodil will bring financial reward for the year. As you pick it, say:

DAFFODIL, DAFFODIL, SUNLIGHT I SEE,
BRING GOLD AND SILVER THE WHOLE YEAR TO ME!

But don't bring just one bloom into the home, bring at least three, or you will have bad luck!

HYACINTH

Known as the first true "perfume" flower of spring, it is no wonder that a hyacinth is said to have a special magic to it. Said to spring from the blood of a youth who was beloved of Apollo (named Hyacinth) who was killed in sport, this flower represents the beauty of youth and the spirit of the sun reborn as love. Its magical powers are said to encourage play and bring success in sports! Give hyacinths, or plant them, to encourage play and frolicking. It is said that when they bloom in a garden, children cannot stay away and games will be played nonstop! If you are an athlete and wish to win, bathe with a blooming hyacinth flower (blue) in your bath, and say:

> Bʟᴏᴏᴅ ᴏf ʏᴏᴜᴛʜ, ᴘᴏᴡᴇʀ ᴏf sᴜɴ,
> Mʏ ᴡɪʟʟ ɪs ᴛʀᴜᴛʜ, sᴡɪfᴛ ᴍᴀʏ I ʀᴜɴ!

Then visualize winning that game or race!

Hyacinth blossoms can also be dried and added to love charms to add playfulness. Keep some in your bedroom to add spice! The dried blossoms can also be kept in a sachet and given to women to ease childbirth pain.

Bɪʀᴄʜ

Birch trees are powerful and sacred trees. Known as the "lady of the woods" because it is the first tree to leaf in the spring, it is also renowned for fertility and feminine power. Erotic rites were practiced in birch groves in ancient times to celebrate spring. Sacred to the goddess Frigga, this tree is also known as the "wedded love" tree, and vows of love taken under it are quite powerful! In fact, giving a branch of birch is a pledge of love, and if returned, a marriage will result. The word *birch* has come down in several languages and means "shining one," "endurance," and "the world." Begin all works of love or beauty under a birch, or plant one to encourage those magical qualities. Place some birch leaves under a baby's cradle mattress to banish all ills and pick some twigs at spring equinox to burn in the house to banish all old negativity and start life anew. Another great charm (after asking the tree!) is to take some birch bark and write a wish on it, saying:

> THIS I WILL BY BEITH'S BRIGHT SKIN,
> THAT MY WISH I SOON WILL WIN!

Make sure to burn it when your wish comes true and bury the ashes at the roots of the same tree.

April

Daisy

The simple daisy has a very romantic history, and there is more magic in that simple flower than you might guess! The daisy is actually the transformed Greek nymph Belides who, to escape the unwanted advances of the orchard god, transformed herself into this humble flower. Therefore it is no surprise that a woman who picks the first daisy blooming and wears it will have men following her with love in their eyes! Yet there is another side to the daisy: It embodies the powers of innocence, gentleness, purity, and loyal love. Sacred to Artemis, the chaste moon goddess, a gift of daisies to a friend means you will always be loyal to each other. It can also call old friends to you; plant daisies in your yard and whisper your absent friend's name three times into the hole before planting and he or she will return to you. Sleep with the biggest open daisy flower under your bed, picked under a full moon, and say this charm to have an old lover return to you:

> EYE OF DAISY, SEEK MY LOVE,
> BY DART OF ARTEMIS FROM ABOVE!
> COME NOW BACK, RETURN TO ME,
> BY BELIDES' BLOSSOM, SO MOTE IT BE!

TULIP

In April, all hearts and minds turn to dreamy fantasies and the ephemeral fancies of new life and growth, especially in the blooming garden! No flower represents these qualities more than tulips. Tulips represent perfect love—something hard to find but easy to dream about! They are said to have sprouted when a Persian youth, rejected in love, wandered the desert crying and each tear formed a perfect tulip. Red tulips embody the power of passion, while yellow ones embody a hopeless love! Other tulips convey different forms of love (use your imagination, because mostly tulips represent that!). They symbolize dreams, fantasies, and desires. Tulips, interestingly, are also said to magically attract fame and banish poverty. If you are looking to start a new business, write a book, or become an actor, you want to plant a number of tulips about your garden. When giving a new performer or businessperson a bouquet, make sure tulips are included, and a gift of bulbs will always be appreciated! For a quick success spell, plant seven tulip bulbs in your garden and with each one plant a penny. Say as you do one line with each one in turn:

Fame!
Fame and fortune!
Fame, fortune, and money!
Fame, fortune, money, and success!
Fame, fortune, money, success, and stability!
Fame, fortune, money, success, stability,
and growth!
Fame, fortune, money, success, stability,
growth, and power!

CHERRY TREE

The cherry tree, in both the East and West, represents the transitory nature of beauty, love, security, and protection. It says, "Life is beautiful, but uncertain." In the East, April is the time to enjoy the cherry blossoms, to sit and drink under the blossoming boughs and recite poetry, sing, and make merry. The brevity of the blossoms reminds us of our mortality and also to "seize the day" and "eat, drink, and be merry." Speaking of which, if you want to know how long you will live, run around a fruit-filled cherry tree three times and then shake it. The number of falling cherries will tell you how many more years you have to go! A cherry tree planted by a home will ensure continual good fortune and prosperity for those who live there. Cherry trees also represent love and have the power to both attract and foretell love! To ensure amorous attention, picnic with your intended under a cherry tree. Another way to hook someone is to stain your lips with the juice of a ripe cherry before kissing him or her. It is said that if you feed your love three cherries from a tree ripe with fruit

(or a bit of wine that has three cherry blossoms steeping in it),
then he or she will fall madly in love with you. If you are lonely
and looking for love, tie a single hair plucked from your head
about a cherry-tree twig, saying:

> BY THIS BLOSSOMING CHERRY TREE,
> ☉ TRUE LOVE, COME TO ME!

May

İris

The iris is a powerful flower in many countries and has so many ascribed magical powers, it is hard to know where to begin! Faith, wisdom, valor, hope, power, communication, and victory are just a few iris attributes! The iris is named after the Greek goddess of the rainbow, and it is said that the iris was the origin of the scepter that kings and queens have used for centuries to signify their royal power to rule. Ancient Egyptians set the iris upon the brow of the sphinx because it personified the magical wisdom of that creature. In the West, the three petals of the flower are said to embody faith, wisdom, and bravery, and so irises should be given to those who have need of those qualities or as a reward to those who embody them. In the East, rice wine heated with chopped iris leaves in it was said to give virility, bravery, and power to warriors. To bathe in a hot bath with three of the leaves and one flower floating in it gives stamina and protection from disease, especially if this charm is recited first:

> SWORDS OF BODY, HEART, AND MIND,
> STRENGTHEN, HEAL, AND FILL WITH POWER!
> TO MY FLESH AND BONE BE KIND,
> THAT I MAY BE AS STRONG AS THE IRIS FLOWER!

It is worth noting that the famous fleur-de-lis is actually the triune iris flower.

LILY OF THE VALLEY

Here is a gentle, sweet flower with a scent known around the world. Its magical powers are only second to the strength of its delightful perfume. This is a flower associated with purity, friendship, and intellectual inspiration. Is it any wonder that bouquets of lily of the valley are often given to friends and lovers all over Europe during the month of May? Mysterious by nature, these are highly spiritual flowers and are often linked with pure (unconsummated) love as well as faith and positive vibrations. These blossoms are said to have grown from the Virgin Mary's tears (in fact, "Mary's tears" is one of its names), but they have been sacred to the feminine spirit long before Christianity. Placing some of the flowers on an altar or by a window with a prayer to heaven will assure it of being heard. The perfume is a powerful aid to any psychic or spiritual work (another of its names is "ladder to heaven"). To lift the spirits and to improve mental clarity, place a bouquet in any room. First circle the room eight times, saying:

> May lily, May lily, clear away
> All that hinders,
> Keep at bay
> All that vexes,
> Evil thoughts,
> Charms and hexes!
> Clear the mind and clear the air,
> May lily, May lily, ☉ spirit fair!

HAWTHORN

Hawthorn, one of the more protective trees you can find, is also called may, may blossom, and may flower! In fact, the famous ship of the Puritans was named after this, and in a way it makes sense because it represents both fertility and chastity as well as protection. What contradicts this, however, is that hawthorn has been associated with magic and pagan beliefs for many centuries. In fact, the Maypole, the fertility symbol that people dance about with ribbons, was traditionally made of a hawthorn tree. Another contradiction in this wonderful tree concerns witchcraft. Hanging a flowering branch over one's door was said to keep all witchcraft away, yet witches are also said to enjoy performing their rites under these trees and even create their magic wands from the branches! One can only assume that these are good nature-worshiping witches! May Day (or May Eve Night), the gathering time of all magical folk, is the best time to sit under a hawthorn if you want to see fairies dance or woodland spirits gather. Of course, the hawthorn drew lovers under its branches on May Day as well, probably because it is called the "Mother of Fertility," and couples desiring children often coupled under the tree on this day, or as the old line goes:

FIRST OF MAY, FIRST OF MAY, OUTDOOR LOVING
STARTS TODAY!

Planting a hawthorn at this time of year is very auspicious and will protect your home from lightning and all sorts of other disasters and problems, as well as protect your animals! Plant the tree, and at its roots place a bit of hair from all the people and animals in the home, and say:

FIRST OF MAY, FIRST OF MAY,
BLESS US, PROTECT US,
COME WHAT MAY!
MAY BLOSSOM, MAY THORN, MAY BERRY, STAY,
ENCIRCLE US ALL ON THIS MAY DAY!

149

Hawthorn is always displayed at weddings, and no wonder! The ceremony in olden times was often the result of the May Day loving under the very same tree!

JUNE

ROSE

Roses denote love and are probably the most powerful love charms one can find in nature! Cut roses, given or brought into a place, create a loving aura, but beware of what color you are using! Here are some traditional beliefs about the magic of different roses.

White—Brings an innocent love.
Pink—Adds happiness to a love or begins a new romance.
Red—Incites desire and passion.
Orange or with orange—Makes the loved one always think of you.
Purple or dark blue—Brings a spiritual karmic love.
Yellow—Beware! This invokes jealousy and envy; of course, you may want to do this!

Wild roses—Bring a wild and exciting love, possibly forbidden and short-lived, but exciting!

Roses are especially powerful charms for midsummer. Roses gathered on this day (summer solstice) are especially lucky, and when dried and placed in a sachet or potpourri, they can be a powerful love spell. Burn a red candle over these freshly gathered midsummer roses and say:

> RED OF LOVE, RED OF POWER,
> ROSES OF MIDSUMMER,
> GRANT MY DESIRE,
> BY MY HEART AND BY THIS FIRE—
> ROSA MUNDI!

The dried roses can be added to red wine, to tea, or to cakes. Soak some in virgin olive oil set in a sealed bottle under the June full moon. Cook with this to add love to anything! If a girl wants to know whom she will marry, she has but to take a nice, dried rosebud and wrap it in white paper. Then she should open it at Yule and wear it. The first man to admire it will be her beloved! Another midsummer rose charm is to take a rose your lover has given you and break it on that day—the louder the sound of the snapping stalk, the stronger the love. To get rid of a lover, burn the rose he or she has given you, but if you want a lover to return, then sleep with the rose for three nights and then heat it dry and burn it—he or she will dream only of you and will be forced to return. Yet another charm is to drink a tea of rosebuds before sleep on midsummer night to dream of a future love. But roses are also excellent healing flowers! To heal any strife, scatter rose petals about the home and let them dry before sweeping the discord away—peace will return. Rose water can be added to the bath or a damp cloth to aid healing and invoke peace.

Peony

Peonies are potent as well as gorgeous flowers, revered in the East as well as in the West for their intense magic and for their beauty. Peonies aid healing, protect people and gardens, ensure happiness in marriage, and make a man virile—all while looking great! What a flower! The flower was named after a nickname of Asclepius, the Greek demigod of healing and medicine, because his mother, the goddess Leto, gave it to him to help him heal the god of the underworld, Hades. Thus the flower has a long and ancient history of healing. Medicinally, peonies were used for everything from coughs to kidney problems, and magically they were almost as powerful, so the ancients say. In the East and West, they are symbols of happy marriage and should always be present at a wedding or anniversary party if possible. Placing them on a wedding bed brings true harmony, and placed in the bath, virility is ensured! Peonies planted in the garden protect it from all manner of evil, and when put in the home, no evil can remain; all bad spirits must flee. To stop unwanted attentions from an admirer, place peonies in his or her path or let dry and burn them. Carrying a peony flower or seeds with you forms one of the most powerful protections from all manner of ill luck and problems. Hang beads made from a peony root about a child's neck or over his or her bed and the child will be safe from evil fairies and other evil spirits.

If you feel a ghost or evil spirit is present in a home or is bothering a person, gather three peonies at midnight and wave them about the stricken place or person, whispering:

> OUT, OUT, TOUT AND ABOUT,
> ALL GOOD, COME IN; ALL EVIL, GO OUT!
> WITH A WHISPER, NOT A SHOUT,
> LUX, COME IN; NOX, FLY OUT!
> AMEN!

☉AK

The oak is the king of trees, sacred to Zeus, Jupiter, Thor, Pan, Dagda—too many gods and goddesses to count! The tree grants power, strength, protection, luck, wealth, and more. In ancient times the oak was probably one of the most sacred trees around the world. Truly it would take a book to do the oak's powers justice, but here are a few bits of lore. The word *Druid* comes from the Celtic name for oak because Druids always met under them because of their power. A source of food from prehistory, the leaves and acorns are excellent money and prosperity charms, and a bough of the tree should be brought into the home on midsummer to bring prosperity. Carry an oak leaf or acorns for protection, to keep old age away(!), and to attract money. Keep acorns on the windowsills to guard against lightning and add the leaves to a bath to increase virility and libido! Getting married beneath an oak is the luckiest place to be if you want a long and solid marriage, and if a couple embrace an oak, especially on Midsummer Day, and say the following, they are assured of conceiving children:

ACORN CUP AND DAGDA TREE,
WITH MY TRUE LOVE I BID THEE,
BETWEEN MOONLIGHT AND FIRELIGHT,
OVER RIVERS AND OVER THE SEA,
GRANT US NOW FERTILITY!

Oaks are closely associated with the sun and the solar cycle, and anytime you wish to bring the welcoming, warming power of the sun into your home, bring in a branch from an oak. To banish the blues, burn some oak leaves in the home. To make a wish at midsummer, write it on a leaf and burn it while peering (carefully!) at the sun.

July

Water Lily or Lotus

All water lilies, and especially the lotus, have been magical symbols of rebirth, spiritual transcendence, perfection, and truth for thousands of years in such widely divergent places as Egypt, China, and South America. Rising as they do mysteriously from the muddy bottoms of ponds and lakes and blooming in pure splendor in the air above, they are said to magically help us focus on the spirit rising above matter. Also symbols of the sun, they are said to purify any garden or place where they are planted or kept. As symbols of meditation, they help us find the inner self with powerful mantras and visualizations. To activate the power in yourself, stare into the open blossom of a lotus or water lily. Breathe deeply many times and completely relax. Visualize reality as the many petals of the lotus surrounding you with forms, ideas, and objects. Every petal is something you think real. Place yourself in the center of the flower, a jewel glowing within reality. Then say, 108 times, the mantra:

⊙m mani padme hum.
(The jewel in the center of the lotus.)

It is said that for a brief time you will transcend duality and become one with "real" reality! This mantra is used by Hindus and Buddhists alike. Water lilies are considered perfect offerings to gods and spirits and were often given to the gods of Egypt when asking for boons; the same is true in Thailand today, where every temple sells the flower. Keep a lotus seed on you for good luck and as an antidote for love spells! If you give a lotus or water-lily blossom or plant to your lover or have one on your altar at your wedding, then your love will always be both spiritual and perfect!

Carnation

The carnation is another flower associated with July and exudes a strong feminine power! Originally from the Near East, carnations have been sacred to the Roman goddess Juno for centuries. In later times it was said to have sprung up from Mary's tears at Calvary, a modernization of these ancient myths. This connection with motherhood was continued when it became the official flower for Mother's Day! Named from the Latin *carnis* ("flesh"), these flowers have very physical powers, it is said! Excellent healing flowers, carnations should be used in spells of healing and given to those recuperating from illness. Wearing one as a boutonniere or corsage will protect you from all sorts of physical dangers as well.

To cast a healing carnation spell for a friend or loved one, gather twelve red carnations and hold them up to the sun and say:

MAGNA MATER—IAO!
TO THESE FLOWERS,
LET LOVE FLOW!
FILL WITH HEALING,
ALL SICKNESS—GO!
BY MY WILL—IAO!
(*Iao* means "heal" in Greek.)

Visualize the carnations filled with healing sun power, then give them to your friend or loved one. You may also let the blossoms dry and add them to a healing potpourri you will give as a gift. Pink carnations indicate a new friendship or love, but never give yellow ones—they reject people. Unless, of course, that is your plan! Give a bunch to an unwelcome admirer or boss and see him or her run!

BEECH TREE
The beech tree is associated with this month, and it is called the "mother of the woods," something that tells you

how very powerful this tree is said to be! The beech is said to have the power to elicit writing and poetry and to grant knowledge and the rediscovery of ancient wisdom. On top of all that, the beech has the ability to grant wishes! On a clear summer day, when the sun is setting, scratch your wish upon a small beech twig or on a piece of beech bark with a knife. Then, circle the tree three times and repeat the following:

> BOC, BOC, BOC,
> GRANT MY WISH
> AS I TALK!
> BRING THIS WISH
> AS I SAY,
> AS THIS BEECH
> GREETS A NEW DAY!

Plant the twig or bark at the base of the tree as it gets dark. By the next day, your wish should be on its way!

Beeches are also associated with books, learning, and finding knowledge. The word *book* came from the ancient term for beech, *boc.* Cathedrals were often patterned after huge primal beech groves, which formed ancient holy places of ritual and learning long ago. To spend a night in a beech grove can help you lose your writer's block and will grant prophetic and/or inspiring dreams. Sitting in a grove at midday will bring inspiration from the gods in the form of sunbeams, it is said. At midnight, go to a beech tree and whisper to it the ancient knowledge you wish to rediscover, then take three leaves. Place them under your pillow, and visions will come to you. Beech trees have the power to bring prosperity, heal communities, and build connections as well. To break down communication barriers, share beechnuts with a group—as you eat them, problems will dissolve. Keep some beechnuts in your cash register or money bag, and prosperity will be yours as well.

August

Poppy

The poppy is such a powerful and mystical plant that it has been ascribed to several months, but most place it as a flower of August. Everywhere the poppy has been planted, it has garnered a reputation for powerful magic! Of course, some poppies produce laudanum (raw opium), and this medicine has been used for pain, sleeping, and visionary work for centuries. This may explain the flower's strong lunar associations and why it is considered the prime charm of dreams, memories, and occult spells in ancient books (like for making people invisible!). Yet the poppy has a mystique that transcends its narcotic qualities. It has been sacred to many goddesses, especially Demeter, the Earth Mother; Aphrodite; and Ceres. The word poppy may come from *popig*, a word with the same root as *pap*. This shows a strong magical connection between fertility, birth, and the plant. Yet poppies have so many other powers! Carry poppy seeds to bring love or fertility. Sprinkle them on a bun or in a soup to give to someone you want to love you, and he or she will! Write a wish on a poppy head and place it under your pillow—your dreams will tell you how to get your desire. If you wish to always remember someone or something, to keep that person or thing sacred in your mind forever, then place a single poppy on your altar and say:

By Hypnos and Demeter, I shall not forget
This wonder (name) that fills my mind!
Held now forever, firmly it's set,
☉ token of Hypnos, always remind!

Because they are tokens of memory, we wear poppies to remember those who have passed on. Yet they are not morbid flowers! In fact, carrying a poppy will bring great luck, and rattling the pods over some cash will attract more of it!

SUNFLOWER

Sunflowers clearly belong in sunny August, and their
alleged powers can almost be guessed at by looking at the
huge, bright, cheerful blooms! They are said to bring health
and happiness, fertility and wisdom! Didn't you just know
that?! Plant sunflowers when you want joy and cheerfulness
to enter your garden. Giving them to friends has the same
effect. They also bring great luck to the gardener and can banish any sorrows. Cut a bloom at sunset and make a wish and
the wish should come true within twenty-four hours. If you
need to know a yes/no answer to a question about a friend or
lover, count the number of petals on a sunflower. If the number is even, the answer is yes, if odd, then no. Want a child?
Eat sunflower seeds, grown yourself if possible. Wearing a
necklace of these seeds will protect you from disease and aid
fertility as well, it is said. Want to be a better person?
Sunflower sap can help! After you cut a sunflower down, taste
a bit of the juice coming from the stem and place a bit on both
eyelids and on your heart. Then say:

I SEE TRUTH, I FEEL TRUTH, I SPEAK TRUTH,
TRUTH AND VIRTUE FLOW THROUGH ME,
AS I WILL, SO MAY IT BE!
IPSOS!

If possible, cut a sunflower down on August 1 or 2 and hang it in your garden for the birds to eat the seeds from, and as you do so, say:

HUNGRY BIRDS, FLY TO ME,
BRING ME MUCH PROSPERITY!

Your garden will be blessed and so will you!

PEAR TREE

The pear tree, its fruit and flowers, are all powerful charms. Pear trees manifest the power of love, lust, and creativity. Also, they symbolize justice and wise government (something we are in dire need of—send a politician a pear tree!). Pear blossoms brought into a home are said to bring long life to the household. To make sure that something is pure, place a pear blossom on it. If the blossom remains fresh, then whatever it is will be fine; if the blossom withers, beware! Planting a pear tree or giving a flowering bough is said to alleviate depression and fear and bring hope. Sacred to Venus, pears are said to incite lust. Burn a red candle and serve sliced chilled pears with a sweet wine to fulfill your nighttime fantasies with a potential lover! Pears have also been emblems of musicians and actors. To encourage such gifts in yourself or another, sprinkle a perfect ripe pear (or a flowering branch) with fresh springwater three times and say:

> POWER OF MUSIC, POWER OF ART,
> BRING INSPIRATION—MAY IT NEVER PART—
> OPEN THE MIND, AND FIRE THE HEART!

Then give as a gift.

To make sure someone is not lying, make a promise or a deal with him or her under a pear tree and all will go well. Keep a wand made of pear wood in your office for similar situations and carry a twig from a pear tree when doing any negotiations, and all will be just and fair!

SEPTEMBER

Morning Glory

The morning glory has always been a symbol of optimism and peace. Its fast growth and the way its fantastic blue, pink, or white blossoms open with the morning sun make it easy to understand this. Yet the flowers, for all their glory, soon fade away, and the vine, no matter how fast it has grown, also soon withers—so we can also understand why morning glories symbolize mortality and farewells. Carry a morning-glory root to lift depression and bring a bit of cheer to yourself or another. Plant them by your door or in window boxes to bring happiness and peace to the home and garden. To remove a sadness, plant one seed for three days straight at the new moon. Each time say:

> MORNING GLORY, FAIR OF FACE,
> HELP ME LET GO OF SADNESS,
> DRY MY TEARS WITH NO DISGRACE,
> TURN MY GLOOM TO GLADNESS!
> PAX ET FELIX!

Because the seeds contain a psychoactive alkaloid, morning glories have often also been considered a plant of the spirit realm. The seeds, roots, and flowers are all said to facilitate visions and all kinds of magical workings, and the vine itself can be used to "bind" things in spells. Place some seeds under your pillows for sweet dreams and give some in a charm to those to whom you are saying good-bye to make the parting less painful.

ASTER

The simple aster has been a sacred flower for thousands of years. The ancient Greeks would decorate their sacrifices with asters, and they were grown about Greek temples, especially the temples to Athena, Hera, and Aphrodite. Possibly this is why they were later associated with love and feminine powers! To gain the love of someone, it is said that all you have to do is get a small thing from him or her and bury it on the full moon under asters or with aster seeds. Water the plant with freshwater to which you have added a tear or a drop of blood and say:

> Sᴛᴀʀ ꜰʟᴏᴡᴇʀ,
> Fɪʟʟ (ɴᴀᴍᴇ) ᴡɪᴛʜ ʟᴏᴠᴇ,
> Bʀɪɴɢ ᴅᴏᴡɴ ᴛʜᴇ ᴘᴏᴡᴇʀ,
> Fʀᴏᴍ Vᴇɴᴜs ᴀʙᴏᴠᴇ!

If the flower prospers and grows, so, too, will the love between you! It is lucky to plant asters on the fall equinox in a garden, especially in the garden of a new abode. The first flower from such a plant should be placed under the bed to guarantee love and pleasure all winter long!

MAPLE

The maple tree is associated with fall because of its glorious foliage at this time. From flaming orange to yellow and blood red, maple leaves are the archetypal symbol of change and transformation. These are also trees of prosperity and abundance. Just as the flowers of September remind us of love in the darkening of the year, so, too, does the maple remind us to save, to protect, and to maintain ourselves and the garden! To protect a newborn, pass the child under the sweeping bough of a maple and he or she will be assured of good health. Maples are great money trees. In the fall, catch as many colored falling maple leaves as you can, saying each time:

> MAPLE LEAVES, FALL INTO MY HAND,
> HERE WILL MONEY COME AND LAND!

Try to catch at least three of them. Place these colored maple leaves around your office, but never let them touch the floor, or the spell will be broken! Plant a maple in front of a new business or give one to a friend who is starting a venture for good monetary luck. Love also prospers under a maple tree. Enjoy a romantic fall picnic under one! Give one to your sweetie for the garden and he or she will always think of you. A plate of food set upon maple leaves will entrance whoever eats of it, like love's first kiss! Send fall maple leaves to friends and loved ones, and they will feel your love and return it as well!

☉ctober

Goldenrod

Although disliked by those with hay fever, goldenrod is a beautiful yellow flower that announces the full onslaught of autumn. This is a very healing plant and has many magical powers, it is said, including the ability to find treasure, incite amorous passions, and bring general good luck. When looking for treasure, hold a long goldenrod stalk, flower out, and slowly turn in a circle, saying three times:

Gold of sun, from whence you come?

Watch carefully—the goldenrod should bow before the direction of your treasure! This can be used today in a different way by simply holding the stalk over various business portfolios or other financial documents! The ones it bows to will be profitable. Treasure is where you find it!

To incite amorous desire in another, brush his or her undergarments lightly with a goldenrod three times and leave the flower in your bedroom in a vase. If you don't have such access(!), then simply stroke your undergarments with the blossom and give it to him or her! The boiled blossoms are said to banish illness and remove a cold or sore throat readily. Sip a bit, breathe the steam, and finally add this tea to your bathwater to banish fall chills or colds.

ROSEMARY

Rosemary is one of those amazing plants (and flowers) that seem to do everything magical! They heal, bring wealth, incite love, and protect from all manner of illnesses and problems! How could we live without it? Rosemary flowers are the only herb flowers noted as belonging to a month. This might be because it is said that if you put a rosemary flower and a silver coin under your pillow on Halloween, you will dream of your future mate!

The flowers, worn, are said to bring great luck, especially in business or gambling. Rosemary flowers even help your mental focus and clarity! A sprig of the flowers will negate any poison magically, it is said, if dipped into food or drink, and wearing a sachet of the flowers will cure dizziness and bad humors!

Rosemary flowers, hung up, will also drive off evil elves, attract good elves, clean the air, and bring health and love to the home or garden—what a flower! To activate this spell, when you hang the flowers, say six times:

Sol invincus! Lux fiat!
(The sun triumphs! Let there be light!)

And envision blinding warm sunlight streaming down upon where you are, filling all with joy.

Rowan (Mountain Ash)

The rowan tree was considered the tree of life by the Celts and Norse. According to the Norse legends, the gods made the first man from a rowan tree that washed upon the cosmic shore; the first woman was made from an ash tree. There is evidence that rowan trees have been used in shamanic ceremonies, magic, and rituals for many centuries, and they have always been on the side of good. The rowan tree is said to have saved the god Thor, and in many myths the rowan is always there to help mankind as well. The Greeks believed that this red-berried tree sprouted from the blood and feathers shed by Zeus's eagle when fighting a demon. Rowans are said to magnify and transmit the Earth energies flowing across the planet on "ley lines"—this is why they have been associated with dragons and serpents (symbols of Earth energies) for many years! To really replenish your energy or to tap into the Earth's power when doing any magical work, simply lean against a rowan, close your eyes, and breathe in the energy. Take a twig with you to sustain you. The dried berries and leaves can be burned in the garden or house to remove even the nastiest bad energies or spirits. If, on the other hand, you wish to make spirits appear (only good ones, we trust!), a small rowan fire in the garden will aid your rituals. All sorts of divination should be done under a rowan tree. Take some of the berries and cast a circle with them for protection and then be still and meditate. You may say the following to get the rowan tree spirit to aid you:

> BRIGIT'S ARROWS OF THE SUN,
> CALL THEE TO THE ROWAN TREE,
> THAT THE TRUTH BE KNOWN TO ONE,
> AS WE WILL, SO MAY IT BE!

Afterward, do whatever fortune-telling you wish to do.

Plant rowans to transform any negative energy into very positive power. Planted rowans guard from evil, provide spiritual focus, and help heal the Earth and all around it! On Halloween the rowan guards the door to the otherworld, and provides access for the wise, between the shadow realms and our physical reality. At this time, boughs of the tree or small equal-armed solar crosses of rowan tied with red thread should be hung over the door of your home or in the garden to protect and empower your space. Remember, it is said a rowan wand gathered at All Hallows' Eve will be a potent magical tool for good!

November

Chrysanthemum

Chrysanthemums, in both the East and West, have been symbols of truth, beauty, optimism, and ease. In China they are also symbols of long life, and in Japan they are the preeminent symbol of the sun goddess and the royal family. Plant these imperial fall-flowering beauties if you want more cheerfulness and relaxation to come into your home or garden. Give them to friends or loved ones to celebrate a victory or to give strength and bravery when it is needed. It is said that no one can lie in the presence of a white chrysanthemum, so wear one or keep one in your office when negotiating or when interviewing others, especially if you are not sure how truthful your clients or coworkers will be!

Chrysanthemums are very protective and are said to soak up bad vibes. Plant them where you feel the presence of a bad energy, where something bad has happened, or where a difficult situation exists. Put them in a room where there has been a fight or give them to a couple having problems, and the flowers will calm things down and remove bad vibes. Rub a blossom on a part of your body where you have pain or other problems and visualize the illness going into the flower, then drop the blossom into a body of water or stream and it is said that the problem will float away as well.

As winter is beginning, the chrysanthemum gives us a last bit of the glory of the summer sun. To cheer up your home with this magic, let some chrysanthemum flowers dry in the noon sun on a hot day. Hold them to the sun and say:

> Sun, sun, come and stay,
> Never, never, fade away,
> Make us smile, make us play,
> By your flower-sun today!

When they are dry, place them in your home. They also make a delightful tea that soothes the soul and fills the home with the smell of summer!

GARDENIA

The gardenia is a romantic and soothing blossom whose perfume is hypnotic and seductive! Just as the chrysanthemum is sacred to the sun, so the gardenia is sacred to the moon, and as such it brings peace and healing and induces waking dreams, meditation, and calm. Sprinkle some of the petals about a sickroom to help healing occur. Having trouble sleeping? Place a sachet of the dried blossoms under your pillow. It is said that any prayer or meditation will be much more effective if a gardenia is placed on the altar first. No low or negative spirits can haunt a garden with gardenias in it or a home with the blossoms near the windows or doors. In fact, if you want to see some evolved spirits of good or attract them to your garden, bedroom, or house, place three gardenia blossoms in a cup of springwater and circle them three times on a night when the full moon is in the sky, saying:

> ANGELS OF GOOD, ANGELS OF LIGHT,
> COME THOU FORTH AND BLESS US THIS NIGHT!
> BRING US PEACE AND BRING US DELIGHT,
> ☉ ANGELS OF GOOD AND ANGELS OF LIGHT!

When you see angelic lights playing about the flowers, ask what you will, but make sure it is nice! Then bid them good-bye and pour out the water. Let the flowers dry, and wherever you place them, there will be peace and calm!

WILLOW

The willow is one of the most sacred trees on this Earth, and it is considered by some to be the actual tree of life. It was sacred to the Sumerian goddess Belili, goddess of the moon, love, and the underworld, and also the deity of water. These themes continue through other willow myths and legends. In Greece, Orpheus, the demigod who visited the underworld and returned, did so with the aid of the willow wand he carried. Persephone, the lunar goddess who became queen of the underworld, also had this as her sacred tree. Hecate, one of the most powerful dark goddesses, had willow groves sacred to her, and thus the trees have been associated with magic and sorcery for centuries.

Willows are said to be "psychic" trees that help you open up your inner mind as well as help you communicate with other dimensions. The Druids, and other shamanic peoples, considered willow groves sacred places for honing psychic powers, fostering visions, gaining eloquence and inspiration, and perfecting arts. Boughs cut from willows, especially on November 1, are great protective charms when carried or hung in the home. If boughs are cut in the summer, then they are potent fertility charms. Want to increase your psychic powers? Meditate under a willow and burn willow leaves in your home as incense. To make a wish, tie a knot in a willow strand and say:

Mother Willow, heed my call,
By this knot, grant my will!
Before thy yellow leaves all fall,
I know my dream you will fulfill!

Any wand cut from a willow will be powerful in goddess magic. It should be the length of your forearm from fingertip to elbow and should be cut on a full moon in silence. If you have been cursed, knock on a willow tree at midnight and the curse will be lifted. If you want love, carry willow leaves, and if your home or garden has too much "fire" energy, or things are too "crazy," plant a willow to bring some soothing, dreamy willow magic into your life.

December

Ivy

Ivy is a powerful plant that induces friendship, great joy, intensity, and intoxication—what a great magical plant to have hanging about your garden! Sacred to Dionysus, or Bacchus, ivy was wrapped about the sacred wand of this god, and it was named after one of his favorite nymphs who became so ecstatic while dancing for him that she died of ecstasy! So, this is the original party plant! Giving an ivy plant is a mark of eternal friendship and good feelings. To ensure a long-lasting love, twine two strands of an ivy plant together in your lover's garden or before you give an ivy plant to him or her. When you braid them, say:

İ AND THEE,
TOGETHER WE BE!
FRİENDSHİP AND LOVE,
BETWEEN YOU AND ME!

Ivy is also a symbol of fidelity and wedded love, therefore a strand of the plant or a potted ivy should be present at a wedding ceremony and a crown made of ivy can even be placed on the bride and groom to ensure fidelity! Make sure ivy is present when the groom carries the bride over the threshold of their home as well! A bit hung on the knocker is the traditional charm. Plant ivy to also ensure against sudden disasters—a little carried in a car or tucked above the door couldn't hurt! To the Celts, the two sacred plants of midwinter (Yule) were the ivy and the holly. Where they grew together, great luck and power reigned. If you can, plant them together in December for great blessings. Pluck branches of them both and place them on your mantel and on your door at the solstice, and nothing but luck and friendship will come to your home!

MISTLETOE

Mistletoe is, of course, the magical plant that forces people to kiss under it—now that is power! Yet this merely hints at its mythic abilities! As many know, mistletoe was sacred to the Druids, and they cut it with a golden sickle from sacred oaks. It was considered a sacred plant of the sun, and this is why we put it up at Yule time, the solstice. Mistletoe was said to have psychoactive properties, but the secret of using this plant to create visions is lost. Yet burning mistletoe as incense is said to aid in gaining spiritual visions, and it is said it will purify anyone and anything. This sacred herb provides mighty protection from disease, lightning, bad luck, and, well, everything! Long after it has dried, keep it in a small jar to protect your home or wear some in a sachet or charm to protect yourself.

Wearing a ring of mistletoe wood will keep all disease away, and a bit hung over a cradle (but out of the reach of kids!) is said to keep children from being stolen by elves. Worn about the neck, it is supposed to make you invisible, but that we have not seen! And, of course, it fosters love. To really make that "kiss under the mistletoe" the active love magic it could be, do this: Maneuver your intended under the plant as it is hanging and hold both of his or her hands, then say:

GOLDEN BOUGH ABOVE,
HERE WE STAND UNDER!
KISS ME NOW, MY DEAR,
BRING US LOVE AND WONDER!

If the kiss is sincere and there is love in it, you will be linked by fiery passion for at least a year! Happy Yule!

HOLLY

"Deck the halls with boughs of holly, fa la la la la la la la la!" So the old song goes, and there is great magic in that spell! To make this enchantment work, the holly must be gathered, with red berries, on solstice morning (December 21 or 22), and a copper coin should be offered to the tree and buried at the roots. Then, say this:

HOLLY KING, BLESS US HERE,
BY THE NEWBORN SUN,
THROUGH THE NEWBORN YEAR,
UNTIL THIS YEAR IS DONE!
GLAD YUL!

Deck the halls and mantel with the blessed boughs you picked, and don't forget to put a piece on your door!

Holly is one of the most powerful trees, especially in Celtic and Norse traditions. A symbol of the "Winter King" and lord of the underworld, it also is said to give great blessings and powers. The sharp, spiny bristling boughs are said to be especially lucky for men, the smooth leaves good luck for women. Holly planted about the house will protect you from all sorts of evil, fire, misfortune, and sorcerers. Today this probably means nasty neighbors! If boughs of this tree are thrown at wild animals, they will back right off. Holly leaves, when wrapped in white cloth and placed under the pillow, will also give good dreams. If you find a piece of broken holly, this will mean good luck is coming. It is unlucky, however, to burn green holly, to pick it after Yule, or to bring it inside when it is flowering.

Holly in your garden and about your home in December will protect you through the long winter and will keep your spirits up and your dreams happy. What more could you ask for? That's why it is called "Holy Tree"! Happy Holly-days!

About the Authors

Sophia is an internationally renowned psychic and a professional speaker. She was taught how to tap her psychic powers by her grandparents when she was a child. At the age of three she began her study of psychic reading, psychic healing, and casting spells. She lives in Seattle with her family and her poodle, Thor.

Denny Sargent is a writer and historian. He is the author of *Global Ritualism: Myth, and Magic Around the World*. His most recent book is *The Tao of Birthdays*. He lives in Seattle with his family and his poodle, Thor.